Memorad

CW01643556

MY SURGEON TALKS TO ANGELS

A journey from science into faith

Dr Veerle Van Tricht

written with Sarah Bullen

Dearest Eva,

The world deserves to see your beautiful feminine side. Shine your light!

Love, Veerle

First published by Dr V for Vitality Publishing, United Kingdom.
First published 2017

Cover Image: Ronel van Heerden
Copy editor: Lindsay Norman
Typesetting: Bonita Barendse

ISBN 978-1-9997138-0-5

Contents

1. Visions and illusions in surgery 4
2. Angels and other beings 9
3. Meeting my first Guardian Angel 15
4. Dealing with my mother 23
5. I am sent away 31
6. The healing awakens 35
7. The dating years 42
8. Making intuitive diagnoses in South Africa 47
9. I feel death 55
10. Back in Leuven 62
11. I finally wake up 67
12. A seeking journey begins 72
13. The beginning of the beginning 76
14. I'm moving on 81
15. Angels in flight 89
16. Fate answers 95
17. Angels in human form 101
18. Astral traveling 105
19. Meeting a soul mate 111
20. Working with my energy 116
21. The flying years 119
22. Climbing the ladder back in Bruges 127
23. I crash and burn 133
24. A downhill spiral 139
25. Modern medicine misdiagnosed me 144
26. A place to heal 155
27. Back in Africa 162

28. A time of loss 173
29. Deportation looms 177
30. Mark goes into freefall 182
31. The first time he died 191
32. Angels hold me 202
33. All alone 210
34. A long way home 213
35. The email bomb 219
36. The gentle years 225
37. Angel messages vs intuition - how do you know? 230
38. Angels I work with 233
39. Meditations and processes to connect to other beings 238
40. Techniques to connect and call on Angels 243

FOREWORD

I know the existence of Angels to be true on a personal level. That is what drew me to this book. I had a near death experience in 2012 and was in a coma for three weeks. During that time Angels visited me. I knew they were there beside my hospital bed whilst I was in the coma journey into other worlds, and they visited many times in the following weeks as I fought my way back to life. They were so real that I heard them, spoke to them and saw them. It is easy to tell myself, years on, that it was a distant dream, or that I had imagined it. However those experiences were so visceral and real that I couldn't diminish them if I tried. So I knew already from personal experience that Angels walk are around us, particularly in hospitals and around illness and death. So when Veerle first told me of her work and her connection to Angels, it seemed perfectly reasonable to me. Why would they NOT be there when a loved one undergoes surgery, or pain or death? Of course they are there! They are there in hospitals in dense Angel packs - it is just not that easy for many of us to see them.

Veerle is unique in that she is a doctor who sees them, communicates with them and actually works with them.

This is not a religious book. Now that seems strange bearing in mind the subject matter. Many people are under the illusion that Angels are linked to a single faith. The clear and concise story that Veerle reveals shows a different story. Her story shows that Angels are everywhere, and they watch over you whenever you need it - even if you are totally unaware of their presence.

She happened to notice them most strongly in hospitals during her work in a hospice ward. She found them visiting loved ones close to death. As a trainee doctor struggling to cope with the physical demands of a hospice ward, this was the last thing she expected to find.

Seeing an Angel is pretty hard to forget and she immediately knew she was in the presence of spirits and Angels. Even though her medical training would allow her to overlook these beings for many years, they persisted in appearing to her. For years she acknowledged their presence, but turned her medical mind to the job at hand. But the voices didn't go away and slowly the doctor started to listen to them. It allowed her to diagnose intuitively just by 'knowing' what was wrong, work with Angelic guidance and to see spirits visiting their loved ones. This deep connection pulled her increasingly further from her traditional training as she integrated the magical and mystical into her work.

Veerle's story is a brave one of a woman who works in a man's world. It is the story of a deeply intuitive soul who is plugged into a greater consciousness and has tried to marry the world of medicine with a personal connection to the divine. It is full of very practical insights into a surgeon's mind as you travel her life of work, love and children.

It is a story to inspire you, and give you faith.

Sarah Bullen
Editor and Journalist

CHAPTER 1

Visions and illusions in surgery

Delusional is a medical term used to describe people who believe they can see or hear spirits, voices, angels or God. I know this term well as I am a doctor. But I am standing in the operating theatre and there are spirits all around me. The man lying under my scalpel is elderly and his long-deceased wife Martha is sitting next to him, holding his right hand. She told me her name. I know I am not delusional.

Angels have been around me my entire life. They were a constant part of my life as a child. Over the last four decades they have come and gone in my life.

They are here now as I stand operating on a patient.

As I walked into theatre just half an hour before, the nurse's CD player was playing Sunshine On My Shoulders by John Denver. The lyrics caught in my throat as I walked past and I felt a familiar shiver down my spine. It was the song my late husband always played for me to make me laugh and cry at the same time, during long car trips through South Africa.

The song was also a bad omen for me and often warned me to watch out. It was one of my many messages from the other realms.

I put my worries aside and got on with the job, but I couldn't shake the feeling it was going to be tricky surgery.

I was right. Not long into the operation, despite the anaesthesia, the elderly patient twitched and the delicate lens capsule detached into his eye. This is not a good situation during eye surgery.

With patients over the age of 80 years old, there is an increased risk of this as the little fibres that suspend the lens in the eye degenerate with age (as do all the tissues in the human body).

This happens: the fragile zonular fibres break and the lens starts tilting southwards.

This is a dreaded sight for an eye surgeon. It means calling for the extra capsular tray, converting the operation into a manual one, cutting the cornea open with scissors and delivering the lens with manual pressure, before it disappears backwards, toward the retina. It is a long and tricky process and it ends with closing the wound with sutures after putting in the intra ocular lens and removing any unwanted vitreous jelly.

This all means the operation will take longer than it takes the anaesthetic to run out, meaning that the patient will soon be in pain and more likely to move.

I was trying to save his vision but now I knew my task was going to be harder to pull off. This is not life and death surgery, but the implications of something going wrong can be huge. It could mean the patient loses his vision.

I shift gear and I move into my private zone, which feels far away from this sterile surgery. I take deep breaths and slow myself down. Then I pray to God and ask Him to surround us with as many Angels as possible. I need their calm and their quiet help now.

Immediately I feel the room change. I feel it fill with light and a calm, comforting presence. I know they are coming. They always do when I call for them.

In seconds the entire physicality of the patient on the table changes. From being agitated under his conscious sedation, he relaxes and his body goes limp. In seconds he actually starts snoring.

I don't need to look up to know there is now an extra presence in the operating room. I can feel her already.

A female ethereal being with long, dark blond curly hair in a long white shirt sits on a chair holding the patient's right hand. She is ageless. She loves him.

Then I sense that she feels puzzled and feels me staring at her. She turns and smiles. Martha is her name. I hear it clearly in my head. She is his deceased wife.

This is not the first time spirits have come into my theatre while I am performing surgery on their loved ones. I see them here all the time. I call on Angels and my beneficial spiritual helpers whenever in need and at the start of any challenging procedure.

I want to tell my patients they are here and that they are protecting them.

But I know that I cannot tell them.

I am a highly-trained scientist. My practice has over 11 000 patients. Since I was widowed two and a half years ago, my three little children rely solely on me to provide for them. It is bad enough that the other doctors hear me pray out loud. I live and work in Hervey Bay - a conservative town on the Fraser Coast in tropical Queensland, Australia.

Martha wants to tell me things. She wants him to know she is there. But to say this out loud would be professional suicide. I am already under a huge threat. I was fighting deportation from Australia a few months ago. Even 3 000 requests from my patients and other supporters in town, the voice of the local government officials on the six o'clock news, and the front page of the newspaper couldn't keep us in the country where two of my children were born.

I can't let people think that I am different. I can't let them know that I am 'The Surgeon who talks to Angels' as some of the nurses once called me. I found out a long time ago that anything that deviates from the scientifically proven in the medical world is rejected. I have been called a witch. My career has almost been destroyed. I know better now than to let people know what I am – a psychic and intuitive healer.

I have lived and worked as a surgeon in Australia for eight years but now I need to pass another test with the Royal Australian and New Zealand

College of Ophthalmologists to be able to continue practicing. My entire professional life is under threat. But it seems to me the most important thing that keeps me sane is this private space I have when I connect with the Angels at my side.

I want to tell my patient that his deceased wife's spirit is here. I want to tell him that she is always there if he needs her. And that she loves him and is watching over him.

But I can't put a foot wrong. I can't allow even a hint of it to get out. I work in a conservative world of medical science and if they thought I was a "woo woo" quack I would never work again. I have fought too hard to build my career and get where I am now. Getting a training place in ophthalmology is for the select few. I studied in Belgium where the competition is ruthless. It takes more than a decade to graduate. It took me seven years in medical school in Leuven, Belgium, to graduate as a doctor. Another four years were spent in Antwerp to become a specialist ophthalmologist, and a further four years in South Africa to become a vitreoretinal surgeon. It took 15 years, a lot of money and tons of hard work to get to where I am now. The competition is even fiercer in countries like Australia, where medicine takes on a more commercial angle. Here students fight for places and patients in a manner I find really sad for the Art of Medicine. But this is where I am working and I need to keep my head down.

So I turn my back on Martha, lower my head, take up the scalpel and get ready to use my medical training to save my patient's vision. But I operate knowing I am guided by Angels – both mine and his.

CHAPTER 2
Angels and other beings

During this book I talk about many different invisible beings and energies that I have encountered over the years. I want to distinguish between them and tell you how I work with each category.

Later in the book I share some powerful meditations and rituals you can do to call on them yourself, including some that you can do when undergoing surgery or any medical procedure. You may find you have already connected with a few of these and you haven't even realised it. Or you may have simply felt a connection to something. Or perhaps you are unaware that these beings and entities are all around you.

The most common entities I work with or recognise are Angels, spirits and residues.

I want to share with you how I experience each one, and how I have come to tell the difference in the way I experience them.

This is not an exhaustive list of all the types of energies, just the ones that I connect with and work with directly.

1. ANGELS AND ARCHANGELS

An Angel or Archangel carries a high vibrational energy that feels like love. As they connect with you, or are near you, the feeling always carries love and support and feels good. An Angel feels positive. You will not get goose bumps or feel chills.

I can almost imagine their wings enfolding me. At times they have actually physically carried me through the air such as during a motorbike accident I once had. You are never afraid when they are around.

One of the key ways you can tell an Angel from other beings lies in the message they give you, as well as the feeling you experience. If you feel fear it is not an Angel! Angels feel warm and safe while the lower entities might make you feel cold. Sometimes I get goose bumps and sometimes the room cools down a few degrees, wind blows through rooms, doors and windows fly open and bang close.

I see Angels as different colours. I see dark green for Archangel Raphael, blue for Archangel Michael – the two main Archangels I work with. I see dark purple for Metatron (a recent Angel to visit me). They look like moving energy blobs, similar to those found in lava lamps but bigger. I see them better with my third eye, when my eyes are closed and when I'm quiet and relaxed - just how I feel during a meditation or healing session.

Your Guardian Angels are always by your side. From before you reincarnate until after you have died and have returned to Source.

2. SPIRITS

These are souls whose bodies have died. A spirit can be a loved one visiting you or just an unknown being that has passed. I also encounter the spirits of my patients and those of their deceased loved ones as they come to support the patient under my care. Spirits, no matter whether I know them or not, almost always feel like lower vibrations to me. At least lower than Angels. When a spirit is near I experience a strong physical reaction. I get goose bumps or my hair stands on end. I may suddenly smell their perfume or just feel them in my presence.

PEOPLE I KNOW

Sometimes spirits of people I have known and loved visit me. My most regular visitor is the spirit of my late husband. I often call on him to protect my children when I am away for a long time, if I leave them with a babysitter, or if they are driven in a car by a young, inexperienced driver. I know he will always show up. My long-term nanny, Katie, mentioned one day that she felt my late husband next to her in the car, telling her to slow down.

Many times during surgery I have felt the presence of deceased healers and ophthalmic surgeons, one of whom I have personally known. They assist me with their knowledge and experience. All of these light beings stand in a half circle behind my back as I perform surgery and speak through my mind and my hands. One I often recognise is a surgeon who was a friend and ophthalmologist in Cape Town who died about 15 years ago in a car accident. I felt his presence for a few years after he died, but then he moved on. Most spirits or spirit guides don't stay with you your whole life: it depends on your mission, on how are you serving the planet and on why you are calling for help.

SPIRIT FRIENDS OF PATIENTS

Occasionally, during a consultation or an operation, I feel the presence of an unknown spirit. They are present for a reason, like Martha who was the deceased wife of my patient. They are here for the patient. Sometimes there is only one, while at other times spirits and Angels fill the room.

I know who they are and why they are there. They come in love. However, the feeling this evokes still makes me feel uncomfortable. As with all spirit energies I get goose bumps and the room gets colder. Over time I have learned to relax with and welcome them into the surgery with love.

UNKNOWN SPIRITS

Most of the spirits I encounter are actually lost souls. I don't know them personally at all. Unknown spirits don't feel particularly good to me.

Some of them are cheeky, and try to talk me into doing naughty things. I feel that very strongly in pubs and casinos, which are full of spirits who cause mischief. Much of the time I want to shut them out. It feels as if they are tugging on me and wanting to tell me things that I don't want to hear. It is not a nice experience.

I don't call them – they simply come and visit me. I have had angry spirits who slam doors and when they visit it becomes very cold in the room. My friend Biebie is very familiar with spirits. The first night I stayed in the guest room in her home the door kept on slamming and the room was freezing cold I was on edge all night. The next day I told her about it.

"Ah, that's my father," she said. "He's just checking you out. He is friendly so don't worry, he will calm down once he knows who you are."

It took a while! But that week the cold breeze and slamming door became less frequent and finally stopped.

I remember one night in South Africa when a doctor friend of Biebie received a phone call that a close girlfriend of hers had not come home after leaving a monthly wine tasting evening. Even though it was dangerously dark and late, Biebie got goose bumps and jumped into her car on a hunch.

She started to drive the road between both homes.

She saw the car immediately. It had rolled off the road. Other cars had stopped to help. Biebie could feel her friend was out of the car, lost and staring at the scene from a distance. Biebie knew that she didn't know she had died in the accident. Her friend is a perfect example of the sort of soul who stays around on the earthly plane. Often they are people who die suddenly and try to communicate with their loved ones. This is beautifully portrayed by Patrick Swayze, in one of my favourite movies, Ghost. Biebie worked hard to comfort her friend. That night she spoke to her: "It is okay to go into the light. Go. You will be all right."

Biebie told her that she had asked her father's spirit to come and support her. "He knows where to go," she told her.

But her friend was not ready. She was panicky and confused. She wanted to stay with her children, which is understandable from a human perspective.

3. RESIDUES

This is a general word I use for an energy that is attached to all objects. This can be a good feeling or negative feeling and it is subtler than other forms.

A residue can be a memory of an intense emotion. It feels denser and thicker than air to me - and it hangs around objects, people or in rooms where it was created by the people experiencing these feelings. You may have felt this in places where it is very strong. You might feel it while walking through old jails where people suffered or were tortured. Or in a museum like a

Holocaust museum where objects and images from a sad moment in history are displayed.

Recently I was staying in my mom's old home. She was not there at the time as she had been moved into a modern care home with friendly staff. My mother cared for the garden and rabbits and was taken on weekly outings and walks through the nearby forest. Truly an example of how the elderly should be treated with loving care and respect. The children found a bag of my African collection of death masks I had brought from a cataract mission in Western Africa many years ago. I also brought home a genuine warrior's shield made from hide, which was too smelly to keep in the house, and Zambezi shark jaws with a plethora of teeth (unlike humans, sharks have spare teeth and can replace any lost ones). I had always felt an extremely strong energy exuding from those African artefacts. I also had a knife that I bought in Cameroon at a market. The owner told me it had killed people and that "It would want blood again". The decoration on the knife was gorgeous. It had a red and white snakeskin coiled around it. That evening in my parents' old house, as we unpacked these goods we all immediately felt the residual energy of a violent death. We all got shivers and my hair stood on end. When my cat got on the table to see what the fuss was about, she sniffed the objects and jumped a metre high in the air before sprinting out of the room. Animals pick up on Bad Mojo much easier than most humans.

My older son immediately felt the change in energy. My younger son, who was only eight, told me that when he opened the bag with "the African treasure", he "got shivers". So that's a good example of what a residue feels like ... odd, scary, cold, uncomfortable, sticky and somewhat heavy.

CHAPTER 3
Meeting my first Guardian Angel

For most of my childhood before the age of six I left my body every night and travelled with an Angel through space. I guess you could say I was an unusual child! I couldn't wait every night to go to sleep. That was the time I would fly around the world.

At this age I hadn't seen anything of the world beyond my street, suburb and country. But at night I flew over the town, out of the country and around the world. Sometimes I even explored our Milky Way and other galaxies.

Most nights it was a conscious choice and I remember deciding before I slept where I wanted to fly that night. As I lay down I would be excited. I wasn't going to simply sleep tonight. I was going to fly. I didn't do it every night. Only the nights I felt like it.

I was never afraid. I was with my friends. There was always an Angel flying next to me, sometimes holding my hand. I saw them as clearly as if they were physical beings. But being so young I didn't question who was taking me or if it was right or wrong. It felt as if my will was taking me where I wanted to go, and then bringing me back to my bed later in the night.

No wonder I loved sleeping. I still do. It is the time when I leave earthly duality and visit the silence and peace of the other reality; the meeting place of like-minded spirits, ancestors and soul friends.

I was six when I met my first Angel during waking hours.

My mother had decided I should fulfil one of her own dreams: I would learn how to play the piano. She even bought me a new cherry wood Rossler wall piano so I could practice every day and fill our home with beautiful music. Unlike violins and saxophones (invented by my fellow Belgian Mr Sax), it is hard to make a piano sound disharmonious. Most of the time, I produced pleasant sounds while practicing musical keys, Czerny and Mozart.

My weekly hour of piano lessons started off by being lots of fun. Every Wednesday afternoon I practiced old and new tunes with my gentle young piano teacher. She wore her long blond hair tied back in a thick braid, Rapunzel-style. As soon as I arrived she took my hands and examined them.

"Beautiful fingers," she said to my mother.

"She should either become a surgeon or a concert piano player," she continued, inspecting both of my hands. "Nice straight and long fingers." My mother couldn't have been less interested in my fingers.
Then she frowned and asked my mother: "Why is this right digit finger bent?"

"That finger was crushed in the car door," my mother said while she looked down at her feet like a dog expecting to be punished for something it did wrong.

The truth was that she had crushed it in the door! It was the first time anyone had shown interest in my finger. But it was clear to all three of us that the subject of my crooked finger was never to be raised again.

My mother came to the music academy that first day only. After that she was never seen there again.

The music lesson was fun, but there was more. Every week I had two to three hours of lessons in music theory and music history. The other students were double my age.

I had just started primary school but I was expected to pass music exams based on several thick, small print study books. I was just learning to read! I loved the music but I could not keep up with the theory.

After a full year of showing up and trying my best to understand what I was being taught, I started begging my mother to allow me to leave music school. I was miserable. But she refused. However, this wasn't the only reason I wanted to leave. I was terrified of something else as well.

The school year in Belgium starts in September, at the end of summer. As the days become shorter, it was already dark outside when I finished my music classes. The main street, De Bergstraat, stretched two kilometres from

the school to my home. It was named after the little hill ("berg" is the Dutch word for mountain) at the centre of town where the church is situated, built in the year 800.
I had to walk home alone in the dark.

My mother was the only parent that didn't fetch her child after class. All of the other parents waited outside until the children spilled out onto the streets.

Her reason? She wanted to be home between 5 and 6pm to be ready with a delicious home-cooked meal when my father came home from work.. Food was the vehicle she used to express her love for her family. Her meals were always delicious but also created a bit of an emotional eating tradition in me. "When I feed myself, I love myself" became one of my subconscious beliefs.

So while she busied herself cooking her meals of love, she left her six-year-old daughter to walk home after music class through the dark streets alone.

I was scared of the street.

One evening, I was all alone walking down the desolate street. The street lights were glowing yellow. The tiled pedestrian sidewalk was shiny from the humidity in the air. My short legs were moving as fast as possible.

The heavy schoolbag hindered my movement.

I walked past a few dark alleys on the way through town. In one of the alleys an older man was standing in the dark next to his bike.

"Come here," he called, "I need your help." I wanted to run but I was scared to disobey an adult. I fought my intuition and walked into the alley. Somehow it has always been difficult for me to refuse to help anyone.

"Have a look here," he said. His eyes were looking at his crotch.

At that moment I saw he was holding his penis in his hand. "I need you to rub this for me. I am in pain," he said.

I froze in fear. As I tried to listen to my instinct that that shouted at me to run, the man grabbed me. Because the bike was in between us, I was able to escape his grasp. The bike dropped to the slippery street and my little body took off like a rabbit chased by a fox. I ran all the way home at a personal record-breaking time. I burst through the door in tears. My mother was home. I tried to tell her what happened but she didn't have ears for me.

"Oh Veerle! I am sure you imagined it," she said.

My pleas to allow me to give up music school or at least for her to collect me in the evenings had no effect.

The next week I had to walk that road again. Terrified and hesitant, I stepped out of the old school building. The street was dark and deserted. In seconds all the other children were collected by their parents. I was left alone.

My fear was so potent I felt as if I was vibrating with it. I closed my eyes and said a prayer to God, asking for help and protection.

I felt a warm hand slip into mine. I looked around to see a beautiful man standing next to me. It was an Angel. He had a glossy shoulder-length blond mane. He was very tall and slender with long arms and fingers.

I say he was an Angel because I just knew it. I can't remember ever actually seeing wings on him but I knew he could come and go without respecting gravity.

I left my hand in his and smiled. I felt safe now and I knew that nobody could hurt me. I walked with confidence at a steady pace and with a smile on my face. He was next to my side the whole way home and he covered me with a cloud of love and protection.

As soon as I arrived at the backdoor of the veranda, he disappeared.

I was never afraid of the dark again.

I knew he would always be around if I wanted him to be.

He was there every time I came out school and he walked me home every single evening.

I enjoyed his presence so much that I continued to go to music school for another five years.

But by then I knew Angels were all around me. I had called on them many times.

One day my brothers thought it would be fun to lock me in the dark and humid basement cellar of our house.

I am the youngest of three by seven years. The age gap felt like a lifetime when we were younger. To them I was a constant nuisance. I was a noisy little attention-seeking girl.

I thought they were heroes. I loved following my brothers and their friends on their adventures through the fields and over fences in our little village. I still remember building enormous snowmen and igloos in the winter. Pulling the wooden sledge down the icy streets was so exhilarating and such fun!

No wonder I was a bit of a tomboy. I grew up with brothers and a disinterested mother who didn't believe in feminine grooming. Added to this, I was dressed in ten-year-old boy's clothes (an early trauma to my fashion and aesthetic senses).

My brothers were distant strangers as children and sadly our relationship never really improved, even as adults.

When I was very young I had to share a room with Yves. But that was no good as I woke every night crying, as babies do. Yves used to scream at me to stop and eventually when I was about two my parents moved me into the sewing room where I slept alone.

That is when I started astral travelling at night, which I share later in this book.

On the winter's day my brothers thought it would be fun to lock me in the cellar, they tricked me into going down into it. They pushed me into the dark cellar, turned off all the lights and locked the door. It was damp and moist and I remember that smell of old, stale air to this day.

I knew they were trying to scare me. Being locked in a smelly room in the pitch dark is a scary thing for a six-year-old girl. But by that stage I already knew better. I knew I was protected and that I could call on my Angel if I needed him.

I had made the link early on that if I was in danger or scared he would show up. This was how I found him that day. My brothers opened the door hours later expecting me to be furious and scared. But I was calm and relaxed, waiting patiently for them to let me out.

I was now so close to Angels that they were my friends. It was totally natural to me.

I knew my Guardian Angel was always there and that I could call on him whenever I needed to. I was so comfortable in the knowledge that I was protected and safe that I hadn't even felt the need to call him that day. I just waited it out.

As an adult I have learned to call and connect with Angels and beings more easily. But while I was learning how to communicate with them I found they came only when I was in danger or if I really needed them.

Maybe this is why I became a risk-taker. Perhaps I had a craving to feel that connection to them again and again. I knew then and I know now that it is in times of need that they will show up.

I gave up music school when I was about 13 and that's when my weekly walk with the Angel stopped.

CHAPTER 4
Dealing with my mother

My parents were both Catholic and I grew up immersed in the deep roots of the Catholic belief. I went to church with the family every week. In church I learned all about Jesus. I liked church a lot. I loved the idea of Jesus and how he made miracles. In fact the idea of Jesus making a blind man see was one of the key reasons I became an ophthalmologist.

It was in church that I also first heard the word Angels. I didn't know what Angels were or where they were to be found. It seemed that, according to what I heard in church, that they were very special beings. But for me they were all around me and they were my friends.

I needed friends in my family.

My mother had a deep love for both of her sons, and her husband. But somehow she left me out of that. I was the one in the family she loved the least.

"I was happy until you came along," she used to tell me.

She had some other mantras that she drilled into me over the years.

I had to give up my job and become a housewife when you were born.

I preferred being a professional woman who could socialise with clients who made me feel appreciated – now I am stuck at home.

I am not happy at home.

Never have kids!

Never get married. You will only become a slave to your children and your husband.

So mine was a fairly cold Flemish family. There was no warmth and no cuddles in our house. Not from my mother, nor from my brothers.

My mother lived in the same town of Heist op den Berg, until 2015 when she died. My mother and father lived next to each other when they were twelve and started dating in their teens.

My father moved away to the next village for years but they continued dating. They were each other's first loves. It was the Second World War and it was austerity and rations. They never let go of this mentality. I was told to wash only once a week. I had to wear my brother's hand-me-downs.

My mother worked as a hairdresser in her mom's salon and my father worked for the government. They started working at the respective ages of 16 and 20 for small salaries, but it was customary for that time for children to give their income to their parents. That changed after they had children of their own. My parents saved up to build their own home so they could finally move out of my mum's parental home.

In the Golden 80s Belgium enjoyed an economic boom. My father's salary doubled and we suddenly had money. We got better food. We would eat fancy foods like frog legs fried in garlic (yum) and crepes suzettes.

My father was quiet and my mother was domineering. I learned to tiptoe around her my whole life. My aim during my childhood was to avoid her wrath.

One story that defined my relationship with her happened when I was just one year old. She put me at the top of the stairs and left me there. She would not come when I called. So I called and called. Then I tried to go to her and fell down 24 stairs. Although I was too young to remember this, I saw it happen during a hypnotic regression. It speaks of my eternal relationship with her – she never listened and never came when I needed her.

I was born in the local Maternity Hospital, which was run by Catholic nuns. I was an extra-large baby. Bless the local general practitioner who managed to get me out without too much damage to either my mother or me. At that time there was only one family doctor and this omnipotent man carried the responsibility for the whole town's lives and deaths.

I felt as if my mother only understood the negative things in life. No matter what I said or how I spoke, she would twist the words and make it seem as if life had dealt her a bad lot.

I saw her a few weeks before she died.
"Mom, you are looking good," I smiled. She shook her head.
"No. I look bad. I am bad," she corrected me.
Her negative words were a constant refrain in my life.

Over the years I have tried to understand her and delve into the psychology of her bitterness. I know that for my mother's first years of her life there was no father. It was a scandal she never quite lived down.

My grandmother had my mother out of wedlock. That was a great sin in those days and she was treated like an outcast.

But eventually my grandmother met a man who fell in love with her and she remarried. I saw him as my grandfather. He was a lovely man. But my mother never felt loved. In fact, she never told us that he was not her biological father. She lied, or rather withheld the truth. I only found out about 10 years ago, after my beloved grandfather died. It was a shame she carried all her life. It caused a lot of strange paranoia in her.

The result was that I had a very unpredictable and explosive mother. She was scary. She had me when she was 36 so when I was a teenager she went through menopause and the combination totally destroyed an already strained relationship.

I was five the night my mother buried eight tiny newborn kittens alive.

I always adopted lost and sick animals. I would bring them home and care for them. I fed them by hand and nurtured them back to good health.

That week I had brought home a pregnant female cat. She was very young and malnourished, a tabby with brown and black patches on a white background. Fifty years ago, where I grew up, adults would find it normal to either dump pregnant animals or throw them in a river, in a bag. These were cruel, cruel times. This generation of parents had survived the Second World War by starving their children and making soup from river rats, once all the cats and dogs had disappeared. It makes my stomach tie in a knot, thinking about it.

Little me, however, was always donating my parent's coins for animal welfare, WWF and Greenpeace.

One night I was sleeping when the pregnant cat came to my bed calling me. She called me to follow her downstairs. She showed me that she had climbed into a box and delivered eight tiny kittens. I was the only one there and I sat in the dark looking at this wonder of creation. But there was one newborn that was not moving. The mother was licking it but I could see it was not breathing. I picked it up and held it in my hands for a long time. I focused my energy on it and prayed for it to live. I rubbed its chest and blew air in its face. Slowly it started breathing.

I was so excited. I went to my mother and woke her up and told her about the kittens. Thinking everything was wonderful and the cats were in safe hands, I finally crawled back into my tiny oak toddler bed and fell into a dead sleep.

The next morning the mother cat woke me. She was distressed and crying, begging me to follow her. I followed her outside where I saw a freshly dug hole in the garden.

During the night my mother had buried the kittens in it. They were alive and trying to claw their way out. The mother cat was in frenzy, trying to drag her babies out of the ground.

I was in shock.

I tried to save as many of them as possible. But my mother came out and saw me. She was angry. She yelled at me and called her father who lived down the street.

I am not sure what he did but they took me inside and I knew that the two of them had killed the kittens.

I was inconsolable.

It made me realise that my mother was capable of killing babies. I was scared of her from then on. Her cruelty had scared me and this small act changed everything for me. I was scared she would kill me. My grandfather was a kind and gentle man but this was what they did in their generation. They couldn't keep the kittens so they had to die.

The incident with the kittens also planted a seed deep in me. I wanted to save things and heal them. I didn't want anything else to die if I could help it. Although the idea had not yet cemented itself into the drive to become a doctor, I knew I wanted to heal people and animals and that became my mission as a child.

My father was no buffer for my mother's moods. He had a government job working in Brussels for the national water company. He worked in a different city to where we lived and he commuted for four hours a day. We only saw him on weekends really. He was creative and fun, but he was absent. He had a degree, which was quite a thing in the 1950s. He was respected and worked hard. We were middle class but slowly he rose through the ranks. He was knighted at the end of his career.

We were so close when I was a baby.

I was only two years old when I travelled on my father's shoulders through art museums and through the Antwerp Zoo. Once a year I got to feed raw peanuts and animal shaped biscuits to the elephants, giraffes, monkeys and other wild animals.

I loved the sound of the waves and the ringing of lanyards against sailing boat masts on the Belgian Esplanade during our summer holidays, and the smell of iodine in the salty sea breeze.

At night my father tucked me into my cold oak toddler bed in the little sewing room with the tiny pink and purple flowers on the wallpaper. It was the best feeling in the world to slip between the sheets and feel that my father had already warmed them with a hot water bottle. I felt safe and loved.

Every night we did the same thing. My father would read me a bedtime story from Hans Christian Anderson, the only children's book we seemed to have at that time.

"Make it a happy ending, Papa," I used to say.

After some initial resistance my father changed the end of the scary old tales and removed most of the villains and acts of cruelty from the story. Before I went to sleep he would kiss me and draw a Christian cross on my forehead with the outside of his right thumb.

Every night he called on the Angels to protect me in my sleep. Then he closed my third eye with the last sweep of his thumb.

He would listen to me when I told him about my nightly visitors. I would tell him the things I saw and did at night. I remember the spirit of a man coming to visit me for several nights, when I was very small. I described the man to my father in detail: "He has a long raincoat and wears glasses like yours." I told him the man wore "a funny hat like a gangster and he never smiles". My father looked shocked. "And he smells like tobacco," I added. He brought out a framed sketch of a serious looking old man.

"Is this him?" he asked me. I nodded in amazement.
"Yes, that's him,' I said. "Oh dad, that is the man who visits me every night!"

I recognised him immediately.

My dad had tears in his eyes and he told me that it was a sketch of his own father who had died recently. My paternal grandfather used to keep big placid Saint Bernard dogs (these are the dogs that are used in the Alps to save people who are caught underneath an avalanche of snow). Just a toddler myself, I loved lying on these long-haired dogs, cuddling up in their fur and riding them like a mini horse. It was a great start to my loving and trusting relationship with animals, including dogs five times my size.

I loved my kind father so much.

But when I was about six our relationship changed. I didn't know why and I didn't understand why my father had changed. Later on someone told me that my strange and complex mother had been hugely jealous of our closeness, even though I was a small girl. My mother had told my father to choose between her and me. He was a man of duty. He chose his wife and he cut me out of his life in a quiet but devastating way.

Losing him was a huge blow to me. He had been the centre of my universe before that. My best memories of childhood were with him.

CHAPTER 5

I am sent away

My saving grace growing up was the fact that my street was filled with other people who provided a counterpoint to my loneliness. My maternal grandmother and grandfather lived in the same street and I visited them every day. Every Wednesday I went to visit my great uncle and aunt who lived a few houses away. They were not religious like my family and it was in their house, that I felt free for the first time.

My great uncle and aunt were very liberal and I got to read political satires at their house. They also handed me a bit of cash "to have a beer" when I was only thirteen years old. In Belgium, beer as well as chocolate, is a staple food. I grew up having half a glass of Table Beer at lunchtime with my parents

When I was 13 my mother sent me away to a convent. Her decision came out of the blue and was to change my life. Her reason? She had found a used condom in a bush near our house.

"You are doing drugs aren't you?" my mother blurted out at me, her face disapproving. She pointed her short index finger at me. Her hands were rough and hard like her character.

"I found this in the garden." She was holding a used condom.

"I don't do drugs and that condom is not mine," I said, knowing she wouldn't believe me.

One of my best girl friends who lived near us had been having sex from the age of 12 was probably the one who threw it into the bush.

"At least someone is having safe sex!" I said. "But it was not me!"

"I know they are selling drugs at the ice skating rink you visit twice a week!" My mother's fury inflamed larger and larger with every argument I brought up.

My heart and shoulders sank. What craziness had come over my menopausal mother today? I feared this was going to be a bad confrontation full of false accusations, drama and unpleasant consequences. This was how it always turned out. After she found me kissing a boy that year she had given me a 1950's book called "Rock and Roll comes from the Devil".

"I find it really unfair that you accuse me of things I have not done! You don't appreciate that I am an intelligent girl and although I have been offered drugs and sex, I have said no and now you accuse me of doing it anyway. You are crazy… Mother, you are losing your mind."

My mother took a deep breath. I braced myself.

"You are keeping the wrong company; I don't want you to have contact with boys. You are going to convent school!"

I froze. My worst nightmare was coming true.

"And if you don't behave on the weekends you can stay there during the weekends too as an in-student."

I felt like throwing up.

If this happened my freedom-loving soul would leave me for the next six years of high school.

Instead of having liberal teaching and supportive teachers at the town's public school, I would be forced into an ugly colourless straightjacket and sent to walk the line with the troops of prim and proper conformist girls. This was so counter to my nature it was as if she had threatened me with death.

My mother followed through on her threat and sent me to a convent from age 12 for my entire high school. My freedom was taken away from me and with it my connection to spirits.

As a young child I had always felt strongly connected to Jesus. I loved the healing stories and for me he was an idol to live up to. Jesus, church and nuns were all part of my life as I grew up immersed in Catholicism. I didn't mind going to church. I loved it. I enjoyed the serenity of being in the ornate old building with high ceilings. It oozed spiritual, high-vibrating energy. I would bathe in it.

But at school I was confronted with the hardness and cruelty of some of the nuns. I equated them with religion and it severed my deep faith.

She thought that locking me up in a prison of religion was an effective way to keep me unaware of the opposite sex. What happened is that it locked away all my connections with spirits and Angels for a very long time.

All my Angels left me then. I forgot about astral travelling at night. I forgot about my angelic escort home and I lived in spiritual isolation for many years.

It took me many years to realise that although I thought my angels left me, the truth was that I had left them.

I shut down my whole spiritual connection: I closed off my love for Jesus (closed my heart chakra). I shut down my natural connection to God and the Angels (closed my crown chakra). I closed my connection to the Divine, to my higher consciousness and inner wisdom (closed my third eye).

I chose to live only in my mind and to study science: Physics, chemistry, biology, history and geography were my new religion. I took it even further and chose to study medicine when I left school. I became a medical doctor.

CHAPTER 6
The healing awakens

It took being surrounded by death to connect with the other worlds again. I hadn't seen or thought of Angels in years. All the years I was at the convent, they had left me alone. And I had left them. I had turned my back on any sense of the divine.

But they were about to return.

I was 20 years old and in the second year of a tough medical degree when I started to see Angels again. It happened in the most likely of places: in a rural hospital, St Imelda Ziekenhuis in Bonheiden. I was working in the critical care wards of the heart unit. It was a progressive, modern hospital set in a green belt with a big lake and forest. It was not far from where I lived. I used to cycle 25 kilometres in my teens to that very lake to swim. I loved that area and I was happy to volunteer there.

As part of my practical work as a doctor I had to volunteer as an unpaid nurse-aid in the unit. I was given a specific job as a junior. I started out doing basic jobs such as taking patients' blood pressure. It was very useful to learn what nurses actually do and how they spent their time. I learned that nurses have the hardest job.

Then I was asked to provide palliative care and bathe and tend to the people who were about to die.

It wasn't the most pleasant job but I was gentle and kind. The patients came in with heart attacks, heart failure or in the last phases of terminal diseases. They were hanging on to life and my job was to make their passing as gentle as possible. Most of those who were admitted were dead the next day. I would tend to them, have a chat, and bathe them.

I tried to make sure they died happily, having being nurtured and cared for.

My first case was an old man who was about 90 years old. I was very young and wearing a nurse's outfit, and I was terrified to be around someone who was dying. The nurses told me to wash him. He was old, skinny and barely alive. I very carefully had to wash his wasted, skinny body. An extraordinary thing happened. As I walked into the room, I was hit by a wave of elevated energy. I can only describe it as feeling as if all the hair on my body was standing up. It was a heightened feeling. At the same time the overall feeling was peaceful and loving. The entire room pulsed with it.

I was very young and hadn't washed an older person before. I was nervous and embarrassed to wash an older man's genitals. Was it too cold? Too hot? But I couldn't talk to him, as he didn't respond. I just took my time and washed him as if I was washing someone who was asleep and who I didn't want to wake. I didn't really know what was going on. The dying process was all new to me. I hadn't experienced how fragile but peaceful people end their lives.

I knew he was dying. I knew it was good for him. But the spiritual energy around me was growing stronger and stronger. I knew that it was all all right and they were waiting for him.

If you asked me 'Who was waiting for him?', I would tell you: his deceased family. It was so obvious to me. They were in the room. His family who had already passed on and also his Angels were there. They were all waiting for him. But how did I know that?

I just did. They surrounded me and it felt wonderful.

I felt as if I was in a warm space that felt like home. It was familiar and loving. I can understand why people who have a Near Death Experience feel like they want to stay there, in the next station, in the Light. It is pleasant. There are no earthly troubles and you can be in a place that just feels light and loving and limitless.

It was strange to be alone with someone in the twilight zone between life and death and to feel this powerful pull from the spirit world.

This man was my first experience with someone who was dying. But working in this unit exposed me more and more to people who were in the last breath of life. At the same time someone from my own world was dying.

So I was confronted with death at every turn. I didn't realise it yet but I brought comfort to people in hospitals. It is why I am drawn to them and I feel right when I am with sick people.

I learned then and there not to get emotionally too close to my patients.

I was devastated when the first few patients died. Then I pulled back emotionally. I gave them my time but I didn't take the experience home with me.

While I was tending to strangers in their last hours, there was a strange parallel in my life. My own aunt lay in the Catholic University of Leuven Hospital dying of metastasized bladder cancer. That was where I spent most of my days as I was studying at that University. So I spent almost every lunch break with her.

Gerda was much more than an aunt. She was more of a mother to me than my own mother had ever been. She was married to my mother's brother but she was the woman who gave me the love I needed in my childhood. She lived two houses down from mine (in an apartment in my grandparent's attic) and her home was my safe haven.

When I was just six years old I walked to their house as usual. It was my daily routine to visit them after school. I was shocked to see my usually happy aunt and uncle sobbing and in tears for the first time in my life. "What is wrong?" I asked them, very distressed at this unusual scene.

"I can't have children," Gerda sobbed.

"The doctors confirmed today that Gerda would never be able to have children because she was born with Spina Bifida," my uncle Julien explained.

"Can I be your child, please?" I asked.

They were stunned. Their faces drooped even more than before. "My mom doesn't like me!" I tried to persuade them. "Is it possible I could be somehow transferred and be your child instead?"

"It is so unfair, because I want a child so badly but you have a mother." She started sobbing again. Julien, who was also my godfather, put his arms around her and ushered me out of the room. "Go home to your mother, Veerle."

I felt so rejected and unhappy as I seriously thought this was the ideal solution for both of our predicaments. She was hoping for a child, I was searching for a loving mother.

Gerda was beautiful, with fine features. She was full and round and feminine. She used to sing operettas with a company. They would put on a performance and travel with the show. They were hobbyists, not professionals, but it suited her extrovert nature.

For a month she lay in the palliative ward just down the hall from the ophthalmology outpatients' clinic where I was training as a senior house officer. As I visited her almost every day I watched as the disease turned her from a voluptuous and vivacious woman into a skeleton with no hair. She loved life. Even as she lay there, knowing death was not far away, she drank champagne and still wore sexy underwear beneath her sleepwear. She was the coolest person I ever knew. But at that stage she had given up, or she had accepted she was going. She invited everyone to her room to say goodbye. She drank champagne that day and made a great party of it.

Her room was different to the rooms of the other dying. I didn't feel the pull of Angels or spirits next to her. I have asked myself often why it was different. Why do I feel the presence so strongly with some people, yet with my own aunt and someone I was so close to, I felt no beings around?

Throughout the years I have come up with a few answers. She was such an elevated spirit her entire life. The difference between the energy in her space and the energy in the rooms of the sad and dying was so different. Whenever she came into a room she could lift the room up and fill it with light and love.

She was an Earth Angel.

What I started to notice was that the Angels and spirits were there to help. Angels were drawn to support and assist the people who called upon them. The emotion that most people call them with is fear and sadness. I have many photos of souls present at fun events, such as the magical light parade in Disneyland. These are the souls that come to surround things and events they love. They are attracted by the happiness and joy in the air. This is why you should never feel bad about having fun after you lose a dear one. They want you to have amazing experiences so they can feel it through you! I wasn't there the moment that Gerda died but I know that some really special Angels would have lifted her away.

My practical work was largely an initiation with death. And in that room with the old man it was the first time I noticed that there was more going on than my eye could see. It started happening more and more. In the rooms of the dying I felt a powerful energy. It was a feeling of peace, love and acceptance.

I didn't have it with everyone and I started to notice the difference. I found that I didn't feel it with the people who were going to live. As I started to notice that, I began to be able to tell which patient was going to live and which would not make it.

It was really strange. I was a trained medical doctor and yet I was relating to the patients on a totally different level. I couldn't place the feelings. But there was nobody I could talk to. In medical school you didn't talk about things like spirits or Angels.

And so I started to straddle two worlds. The biggest part of me struggled through the science of medical school. I was immersed in science and exams and practicals. I tried to ignore these strange and powerful feelings.

The other part of me could not stay away from the connection I felt around these wards.

It was only when I walked into a ward that I was drawn deeply back into these feelings. I felt the connections most deeply when I worked in the older hospitals. I loved the energy of the spaces. They were filled with Catholic nuns in long robes bustling about and a feeling of love. I felt it and I loved working there. I felt the peace coming from prayers in the chapel, filling the halls with a healing and comforting light.

I knew my future lay in the modernity of science. But on every quiet day I would find my way back to the older clinics where the deeper magic pulled me closer.

CHAPTER 7
The Dating Years

Between the ages of 16 and 27 I dated the same guy. He was a dreamboat.

Once a year, all the teenagers of my Flemish hometown got treated to a disco in a communal hall. My childhood girlfriend Myriam and I were dancing like the freedom-loving Pisces we both are, celebrating life through movement and music. We wouldn't leave the dance floor from the first beat until the moment we were collected by either Myriam's father or my brother.

I was 14 when Geert, my second boyfriend, courted me. The relationship lasted only three brief months but he introduced me to a magnificent group of friends. They were not to leave my adventurous life for a very long time.

After three months Geert broke my heart and our relationship. But he led me to my long-term love.

One Saturday night, soon after our breakup, I had a strange calling to leave my house. I climbed out of the first floor window of my bedroom. I had no real idea where I was going and I was in a trance-like state.

I climbed down the tree next to my window and in the full moonlight rode my bike to a dark forest at the other side of town. I had no real idea where I was going.

After leaving my bike against a tree, I walked up the dirt road towards the sound of music and lights.
There, in the middle of the forest, was a dark rock and roll beer garden in the cellar of a restaurant.
I woke up from my trance in front of the entrance.
"What am I doing here?"
Then I recognised it as the last place I had visited with Geert.
"Is that why I am here?" I wondered "Am I to reconnect with my lost love tonight?"

As I stood there feeling confused a slightly familiar figure walked out in the dark.

It was the brother of a mutual friend. He was surprised to see me.

"What are you doing here?"

After all, I was only 14 years old and out alone in a dark forest.

"I am looking for Geert. Have you seen him?"

"I think I saw him inside," he answered.

I was scared to go in, suddenly feeling very shy as the only teenage girl amongst adult bikers as well as longhaired hippies.

"What if I don't know anyone in there?" Or even worse: "What if any of my brothers are in there and tell my mum!"

The Beach Boys and Thin Lizzy's sounds lured me into the den.

The place stank of stale beer and I froze to let my eyes adapt to the disco lights. I searched for any friendly faces. I got some curious looks from the regulars as I was drawn towards the back of the room.

His white shirt stood out in the fluorescent lights. The collar was buttoned all the way up and perfected with a narrow black leather tie.

This guy had style and I was immediately drawn to him. I felt butterflies in my stomach but I pushed those feelings aside with willpower and loyalty to Geert. I didn't realise it in that moment but this was a destiny date pre-orchestrated in heaven. There was a tingling on my crown from my Guardian Angels, but I chose to ignore it. But I knew without a doubt that I could trust this guy. His hazel brown eyes noticed me, and he smiled shyly. He had brown hair and a pale face. His whole look shouted "my mother chooses my clothes and hairstyle" a bit too clearly. Luckily his mother (who would become a dear friend of mine and substitute mother) had good taste and style.

He was one of Geert's classmates and friends. For the purposes of this book I am going to call him Johan, after my first boyfriend of three weeks.

I pulled his black tie so I could talk in his ear, as he was a lot taller than me at 1,82cm. Of course I was flirting!

"Have you seen Geert?" I aimed at his left ear.

"He was here earlier on, but he left." Johan answered with a one sided apologetic smile.

"Do you know where he went?" I asked deflated.

Johan shook his head while he sipped his Coke through a straw.

"Real guys don't drink through a straw," I said cheekily. Not many people could take my sass but Johan was strong enough to take it. He removed the straw and drank from the glass.

"Is that so?" he asked with smiling eyes. Even though we were not consciously aware of it, I met my soulmate in that moment.

We stared at each other while the music blurted seventies music.

When La Bamba came on it was time for a ritual I hated. It was the cue for pimply nerds or shy young men to kiss any girl they wanted to. I was not a fan of this ritual of being kissed by strangers. Sometimes they would even swing you around so you lost balance and they would catch you on one knee, like a gallant knight, before they slobbered on you. It was also the moment during every tea dance evening that the renegade boys grasped the opportunity to touch any blossoming girly bits. I did my best to avoid this ritual by hiding in the toilets or behind the bar.

This time Johan and I both watched and laughed. We became good friends from there on. We spend most all our free time together going out to discos and movies every weekend, enjoying relaxed beach holidays in summer, looking for chestnuts in autumn and skiing in winter.

Johan was four years older than me and he had a car! A major asset for a freedom-loving teenager like me.

On my 16th birthday he gave me a single red rose, with its stem wrapped in aluminium foil (so it would last longer in the booth of his silver Ford Fiesta) and a bottle of Port.

Then he kissed me.

I believe we make soul deals to meet each other on earth, before we are born. It was the same with Johan.

The two of us were inseparable after that. We were to remain that way for the next eleven years. We lived the high life. Cross-country skiing in the Ardennes in winter, going to the beach in his uncle's Porsche in summer, family dinners and holidays… or we went on adventures all over the country and beyond. We visited the East Coast in the United States, Thailand, South Africa, Spain, Italy and Corfu. Or we just spent time hanging out with each other at his parent's home.

Johan was the man any mother would wish for her daughter. My mother had no such kind wishes for me - but I chose him anyway! He was good looking, generous, handy and sophisticated. And he liked me.

He was a Leo so he loved to party – just like me. He also gathered a lot of female attention around him, like a pride. That part I didn't like, it made me feel neglected. I was too young and insecure to deal with it. He was quiet but stylish – and he communicated fluently in four languages. His family had a wealthy business and he took it over shortly after college. He had access to the family's Ferrari and Porsche and more luxury cars. He was sophisticated and urbane and girls loved him.

Unfortunately he also liked attention from other girls, but it took me a very long time to realise that!

CHAPTER 8
South Africa and Intuitive Diagnosis

The sixth year of my medical training was an elective year. We had to do four months of surgery, four months of internal medicine (non-surgical) and four months of obstetrics and paediatrics. I did the first eight months in Belgium.

For my last four months I ended up in the most unlikely of places: South Africa.

It was destiny of the best kind, and it came about in a totally seamless and simple way. I realised after the fact that I had put all the events into place already.

It was the end of the year and all the medical students hired the entire opera building in Leuven where the final year's students did a comedy skit on the professors. I went with a girlfriend to watch the concert and it was a hilarious, fun night. During the break we went to the bar. It was packed and we were all squashed up against each other.

I overheard someone say, "It was so fantastic in South Africa."

It was a guy I didn't know but his conversation captivated me. Just the words, "South Africa", sounded so exotic. It drew me immediately. My friend started talking to him. He told me about his elective year and he told us why he had chosen to go to South Africa. As he spoke I remember feeling my heart beat faster.

I knew that was something I wanted to do.

So from that very night I knew I was going there.

It wasn't easy getting there and I had to pass a tough medical English exam to be selected to do part of my practical training in South Africa. But I passed them all and kept moving towards my goal.

I arrived in South Africa to do my four months of practical training during the dying embers of apartheid. As I landed in Cape Town I felt excitement build in me. I had this feeling ... I am home.

The year was 1992 and I could not have chosen a more dramatic year to live in South Africa as it was the most politically-charged time in the country's history. Apartheid was a system of racial discrimination and segregation in the South African government. It was formalised in 1948, forming a framework of political and economic dominance by the white population. It severely restricted the political rights of the black majority. The apartheid system in South Africa came to an end through a series of negotiations between 1990 and 1993 by the De Klerk government (De Klerk would later win the Nobel Peace Prize with Nelson Mandela). Against the backdrop of political violence in the country, 200 deaths were recorded between July 1992 and June 1993. The tension was tangible in the air between the races. The stress and refrained anger was visible in the faces of mainly coloured kitchen staff and nurses in the hospital.

These were exciting times for mankind and it was a time that South Africa was one of the most exciting places in the world to live. South Africa relatively peacefully transitioned into normalising the rights of all its rainbow-coloured people. It was called the Rainbow Nation and I was a part of it!

I was so excited to witness this turmoil and elation first hand. When the vote came in that would give black population the right to vote most of the country threw a party. It was a big step forward. The African National Congress, the ANC, won the first non-racial election and Nelson Mandela (my hero) would become their first non-white president. The air was alive with excitement.

I was living in the heart of Cape Town doing two months of obstetrics and gynaecology at Tygerberg Hospital.

I was put in a flat that I shared with two male students. We lived next to the hospital. Early on we decided to buy a very old car that we could share. On our first weekend out we crashed the car into a police car. We were taken straight to jail. It was the first of many calls our Professor would get to help us out of trouble.

When you do your practical training as a doctor in South Africa you are thrown in the deep end. They show you a procedure – such as delivering a baby – once. Then you are expected to do the next one. It was a case of 'watch one, do one, teach one'.

After a single delivery I was put in a position where I had to deliver a baby the next day. I didn't really know what to do. I had never had a baby and I hadn't watched a delivery before now. But I felt my Angels surround me and this made me act so calmly. I felt their love and support. I was loving and gentle.

It was a jam-packed maternity ward. Most of the pregnant ladies didn't speak English and I didn't speak Xhosa, but the nurses were there to assist and it all seemed to just work.

The system worked like a well-oiled machine. When a pregnant woman was in labour she arrived in the emergency ward. She was put into a delivery room as the labour progressed. The nurses handled it until just before delivery and then they called a doctor. I came in to do the actually delivery. I walked in and made sure the birth went well. If all went well the baby was delivered and I left the mother with the nurses.

If the delivery was complicated the case was escalated and the mother was booked into a C-Section.

I noticed some small, eye-raising practices. One was that doctors occasionally clamped the tubes of an older woman without her knowledge. These were older women with around ten children. The doctors would quietly just do this. At the time it was a shock but I believed that this was done to save the woman's life. These women were at risk of carrying another child, living in poverty and refused contraception due to a cultural lack of understanding.

They always offered contraception first but many women refused – either not understanding the idea of preventing a pregnancy or it was against their belief systems.

For my last two months of my practicals I moved to the world-famous Red Cross Children's Hospital.

The Red Cross sat at the foot of Table Mountain and its halls carried the pain of so many riots and deaths. It was a huge heaving mass of people who streamed through its doors every day and night from all the surrounding areas. I felt a big heavy energy there. There were so many people who were not happy. I felt the pain in a dark and heavy way.

It was a multiracial specialist hospital for children. It was packed with Aids babies. It was the first time I was confronted with that. I had never seen Aids patients and the wards were full of terminal babies. This was before HAART (Highly Active Anti-Retroviral Therapy, an old-school name for HIV treatment) treatment so the babies were abandoned or dropped off at the clinic. Their lives were short. Once they got an infection I knew they would not live. They had no immune system.

My job was to examine them every day and to check up on their health. I had two favourites that I could not leave. One was a six month old and the other about two.

I stayed in the nurse's home next to the hospital. It was cold and wet in winter and not very nice. The accommodation had several floors and I was at the top. Each floor had about 20 rooms and at the end there was a communal bathroom. It was winter. It was so cold and there was no heating. I used to run a hot bath and sit in it for hours. I had just done a scuba diving course and this all worked very well. I would climb into my bath with my mask and snorkel and lie there practicing my breathing. The good thing was that it was a short walk to work. I rolled out of bed, walk downstairs to a warm breakfast of mielie pap (porridge) with full cream milk and sugar.

I had a lot of free time so I spent most of this watching surgery. I watched as ophthalmologists examined and worked on children. I volunteered for night shifts and weekend shifts. I wanted to learn all I could.

I was like a sponge absorbing everything.

I was also fast getting a reputation as a quick and competent doctor. Mostly I was getting known as making quick and accurate diagnoses. This is really important as a doctor.

I was in my element working in emergency and diagnostics.

But my diagnosis came from a different place to other doctors. I knew what was wrong with the patient. I knew it without medical records or tests. It was as if I just immediately would know or see what was wrong.

Often the professors would test us during rounds. They would present us with a case and not allow us to see the diagnosis.

There was one child the professor presented to us during a teaching round that stumped everyone. He had a limp and was seven years old. His mother left him at the hospital and never came back. He could hardly walk and he was getting progressively more immobile. The professor made us all look at him as he stumbled through the room.

"What do you think is wrong with him? What is your diagnosis?"

Everyone said their piece giving reasons.

I disagreed.

"He is not paralysed. This is not a physical thing. This is emotional. He can't walk because he has emotional issues."

The professor smiled.

He knew this all along. They knew that the child did not want to be in that family. They suspected there was abuse and the small child had created a psychosomatic paralysis to get out of his house.

Of course I was a trained doctor and I had the medical information all in my head. But these answers came to me in a different way. They came as direct messages. I first noticed this in our practical exams. We were given patients and had to make laser-fast diagnoses. I always got them right but I confused my examiners. Unlike the other doctors who went through thorough exams, tests and analyses – I just got the answer with seemingly little evidence. I was told that I had the answer right but they didn't know how I got there. The truth was that I just knew! I heard or knew what was wrong. I am a medical intuitive.

By then I was becoming more and more aware that I had some healing talents that went beyond my ability to see Angels by the beds of my patients.

I was in my element working in emergency and diagnostics. When I am alone with a patient I connect very quickly with the messages. I know or hear what is wrong and can make a quick diagnosis.

I also was amazingly good at fine surgery. Before the elective year we had never actually sewn human tissue. But it was as if I knew what to do. The doctors were amazed, saying they were sure I had done this many times before. But when I stood there with sutures I felt as if I was guided.

I was guided. As always Angels were by my side.

In Africa I felt different Angels to the ones I was used to feeling and seeing. The energy was raw and grounded and earthy there. It was a turbulent time in the country and the entire population was living in fear as a political system was in its dying throes. African people were rising up, angry and ready to move into a new world of politics. There were riots and fights on the news every night.

Africa felt like survival and angst. It felt like crime and life and death. If felt like I had to walk through dark clouds. But the pull was intoxicating. It was raw and honest and I felt magic all around. It was also a land of such contrasts. There were times when the energy of the people was so light I wanted to float away on it.

African singing and chanting is intoxicating. It rises above you and it calls spirits in its path. The feeling is high and light.

I even connected with the energy of Mother Earth in South Africa. It may be a cliché but I always see Mother Earth as an African woman - large and fat and fertile. I feel this energy in its nature. It does reach out for higher consciousness.

CHAPTER 9
I feel death

I had been away from Johan for four months while I was in South Africa and I wanted to see him. I was feeling distant from him and I was hearing rumours of a blonde he was spending a lot of time with. I thought it was time to spend some time with him again. So we planned a holiday and he brought two of his best friends to South Africa. We planned the entire thing, every detail. We would do a road trip up from Cape Town along the Garden Route all the way up the East Coast of South Africa.

I couldn't wait to show them the coast with its wild seas and huge surf. Earlier in my practical I had visited the small village of Cape St Francis where my professor had a beach house. It is a small beach town on the East Coast of South Africa. For most of the year it is half deserted, with only retired couples and the odd holidaymaker passing by. But every December hundreds of holidaymakers flock there from the inland towns for the warm waters and the long stretches of beaches. It sits just north of well-known St Francis Bay. But the entire stretch is best known for one thing – it is one of the best surfing spots in the world.

Professor Odendaal was the head of obstetrics at Tygerberg. We all stayed in the residence next to the hospital and he lived with his spouse in a flat next door. He was a very fatherly, friendly figure and I was close to him and his wife. He was friendly with all the foreign students but he had a soft spot for Belgian students. He had also visited Louvain a few times and knew it, so he looked after the Belgian students particularly well.

He took me into his family with welcoming grace. I got even closer to them as he had two friendly daughters my age. I had been lucky to visit his beach house before, with his family. This time we were just stopping in for a night on our way up the coast.

We arrived in the morning and Johan and I went for a walk on the beach. The sun was shining and I was with my boyfriend in the country I loved so much. It was the best day ever. I was in love and happy to be alive. We strolled hand in hand on the beach, waves refreshing our feet, the warm sunrise caressing our skin. I was so grateful to be alive and living in the most beautiful country I knew: South Africa, in the year of 1992.

In the afternoon my friends and I followed the professor's children to the local surfing beach. The waves were high, the sun was warm, the salty spray was calling me. The boys decided to have a nap on the beach.

I wasn't going to try my hand at surfing – that looked far too challenging for me that day. So I borrowed a body board and tried to catch a few waves closer to shore. It was amazing. Time after time I swam out holding the polystyrene board and chased a wave. Then I rode it into shore, absolutely loving the power of the ocean. I must have been swimming for close on an hour when I became aware that I was quite far from shore this time. I started to kick back, thinking I would catch a wave to get back. But I was being pulled out to sea.

I kicked harder. But I was making no progress getting any closer to the beach. In fact, the shore was becoming further and further away. I was being swept out to sea. I tried to stay calm. The waves were big but I couldn't seem to catch one in. Then I made a big mistake.

I thought I would make more progress if I let go of my board and tried to swim to shore. Surely a hard swim would take me closer – I could use both my arms and legs rather than just kicking on the board. So I let go of my board and started swimming.

As soon as I let it go, I realised my mistake. The sea was rough and I was suddenly in it, rather than floating above it. I could feel I was caught in a powerful current. But now I was also victim to the tumbling waves. Wave after wave pounded my body down toward the ocean floor. I was tumbling around like clothes in a washing machine, my skin scraping the underlying coral. For eighty percent of the time I was underwater. I knew already I was fighting for my life.

Every cycle my mouth surfaced just long enough for a short gasp of air like a fish coming out of the water.

"COME ON Veerle!" I told myself. "Just stay calm and someone will see you are in trouble soon enough." A month earlier I had done a diving course in Cape Town and I knew the international emergency signal. I waved my extended straight arm above my head to try and get someone's attention. It was futile. I was so far from shore now that nobody would see me. Was anyone even looking for me?

When I did my dive course they had shown me how to hold my breath and to stay calm in distressing situations. I had to dig deep and call on this training now. I had one idea in my mind and one only – just keep your head above the water.

My battle was purely physical. For a girl who had spent a large part of her life talking to Angels, the only thought in my head then was of pure survival. Breathe. Swim. Breathe. Swim. Breathe.

I did that for half an hour and all the time I was drifting further and further along the coast. I was getting close to an area one of the kids had pointed out earlier that day: Shark Point, a coral reef surrounded by seals and their predators: sharks.

At that point I was so exhausted that I was ready to give up and die. I decided I would rather die than be a shark's lunch. I saw my life pass in high speed in front of my eyes: so much love, so many adventures, friends and fun.

I felt very grateful for the decisions I had made in my life that lead me away from conformism and closer to myself. No regrets … I realised that only my grandmother would be sad if I didn't return "Tourist eaten by sharks at Cape Francis" I imagined the front page of the local newspaper would say. Perhaps it wouldn't even make the front page. I could be buried a few pages into the paper.

Thinking of my grandmother reading this summary of my life gave me a sense of determination. No. Hell no! I was not going to die now. I could not let my grandmother down.

I told myself I wasn't going to have an early death by drowning in South Africa.

Then I turned to God.

It was one of the first times in my life I have addressed him directly. In fact I hadn't had much of a conversation with him before. Apart from attending church I had never felt the need for God in my life before. I had always been surrounded by Angels that I assumed came from him in some way.

But that afternoon His was the only presence I called on.

"Dear God," I pleaded, "I know that I haven't been to church much the last seven years, but I hope you don't take that personally. My whole life I have honoured your presence in nature, animals and humans alike."

I lay there in the ocean, holding on to life, and I made a promise that rang true to the core of me.

"Could we agree on a deal, please God? I am not going to promise that I will go to go church every day. That is not my style. But if you save me I promise you that I will be a vessel for your healing. I will continue the rest of my life in your service if you save me now."

"I don't have much strength left in me. I can't hold on much longer."

I lay back in the ocean and stared at the sky. I was totally alone. I was going to die and nobody would even know. But then a movement caught my eye on the sand dune in the distance. It was a surfer standing surveying the sea and holding his board. He was about 20 with dark blond curly hair and wearing board shorts.

I was too tired to even hope. I was sinking. I was too tired to fight. I was ready. I was ready to calmly accept my death while trying to be grateful for an awesome 25 years on this beautiful planet.

Then I heard a shout.

"Swim towards me!" The young surfer was approaching me, paddling closer on his board.

I shook my head.

"Can't." I went under.

I felt a hand on my shoulder dragging me up.

"Get on the board!" He had grabbed my shoulder with one hand while holding onto his board with the other.

Waves continued to crash over both of us. But he held on tight to both his board and me. We tumbled in the rip in a threesome with his surfboard also handing out some knocks.

"I am too tired," I whispered, completely drained.

"Do you want to live or not?" he shouted.

"Yes, I do," I nodded, tears running down my cheeks.

"Then get on this board NOW," he commanded.

He dropped in the water and lifted me on his surfboard. Absolutely limp, I clamped my hands onto the sides of the board and I knew nothing would get them off.

It took him another 30 minutes to get us out of the rip towards Shark Point Rock. We got out of the sea and I collapsed on the beach. I couldn't speak at all. I was too tired. He took me to my concerned friends on the beach and was about to jog off when I grabbed his hand.

"Thank you," I whispered. "You saved my life."

He grinned.

"No problem," he said.

I asked his name and he called it over his shoulder as he ran back into the surf.

"Michael."

I never saw him again.

That night I was so angry with Johan. My fear had turned to anger. Why had he not looked for me that morning? He had been sleeping on the beach, without a care in the world, as I was dying just metres from him. I was so angry. He was confused. He didn't understand my rage for him. I didn't understand it. But it felt wrong. It felt as if he should have felt my distress; he should have felt it somehow. But instead he had been casually sleeping right there in the sun.

Actually, things hadn't been so great with him. As he walked towards me off the plane I felt that he was not sure. I knew something was up. What I didn't know was that Johan had started a long-term relationship with the blonde girl. It was a relationship that would haunt me for years to come. This blonde was going to remain in our life for a long time.

I made a promise to God and to myself that day that I would use the gifts I had barely begun to notice. I think that from that moment on my life had a purpose. I wasn't aware of it at the time. I was just a young doctor trying to do her best, pass her exams and make a career. But something had started there in that ocean that chose my destiny.

It took me almost six more years before I started living out that promise.

My practical trimester in Cape Town was coming to an end and I knew it would soon be time to head back to Belgium. The thought was not inviting. I loved the warmth and the sun of Africa. I loved the people and the energy of the earth here. I had felt so alive.

CHAPTER 10
Back in Leuven

I had now been studying medicine for six years and I had another to go in order to qualify as a medical doctor. So during 1993 I had to spend another year at the Catholic University of Leuven to complete the last year of my degree. This was my seventh year of studying and it was the year we could try a specialisation for six months. After that I had another four years of studying ahead of me.

I chose ophthalmology as my specialty.

I had from a young age held onto the fable of Jesus being able to make a blind man see. But another reason was more close to home.

I was near sighted like my whole family and needed to wear glasses constantly from the age of six.

This meant yearly visits to the friendly local ophthalmologist for updated spectacles. I spent a lot of time in his waiting room as he was extremely busy. I told myself: "This man needs some help! This town needs another eye doctor!"

It most likely all played a role in my preference for this fine specialty where we work with tiny instruments through a microscope. It was the most high tech specialty and still is. We use several kinds of lasers, surgery, implants, transplants, eye drops and injections to treat a plethora of different eye conditions.

The eye is the only organ where we can look directly at a part of your brain. Your eye nerve has one million fibres that radiate outwards in each retina. We can also assess the hardness of your blood vessels by looking directly at them through your cornea and lens. This is very helpful to grade the severity of cardiovascular damage caused by high blood pressure or diabetes. Sometimes the retinal arteries get cholesterol embolisms, which we try to move on. Other times the arteries and/or veins just close up and cause a stroke in the back of the eye.

I applied for ophthalmology but this was one the most coveted specialties. I was accepted in Antwerp under the condition that I work a year overseas first. So I had to do a roundabout route to get into the field. I sent letters to all the universities in Europe.

I was selected to do the first year of my specialisation in Paris at Le Foundation de Rothschild.

I was ecstatic to be accepted there but this meant I had to learn to speak French really fast. So I made that my mission. I had studied some French over the years but I knew it was not enough. I listened to every conversation on the metro and tried to figure out what the locals were saying. The advertisement boards along the route helped me read French better. I listened to French music and watched French TV. In three months I was speaking conversational French – as fast as the Parisians.

In February I got an amazing opportunity. I went for a month to Cameroon with Medicines sans Frontiers (Doctors without Borders). A colleague was going but he dropped out at the last minute and they suggested I go instead. I had never done cataract surgery before so they gave me a crash course and I did a few small procedures.

So I got on a plane to the African country with clear instructions from my Professor Madame Aron-Rosa: "Please don't do too much surgery."

The clinic was rural and remote and hot. I barely slept the entire month I was there. If I turned on the light the floor was black with insects. I had to shower about eight times a night to fight the heat. I had constant diarrhoea. There was no clean drinking water so I drank Coke from recycled glass bottles the entire time I was there, thinking it was safer.

When I arrived at the clinic, there were queues of people with white pupils, totally blind because of cataracts (a white cloudy lens). So I ignored my professor's instructions.

I wasn't a totally free agent. The local Cameroonian nurse controlled the show. He had four wives who each lived in their own huts and he ruled the clinic. He was also having an affair with the young blonde French optometrist who had been working there for two years. He was very intelligent and smart and he actually even performed the surgery himself while I was busy consulting patients in the clinic.

There wasn't a day without adventure in the clinic.

There was one old and confused lady amongst the ones I operated on for cataract who I won't easily forget. She was agitated and didn't speak French so I couldn't understand what she was saying. As I took the opaque lens out, the light from the operating microscope shocked her. I delivered her stone hard black lens through the corneal incision and replaced it with a PMMA lens (poly methyl acrylate is the same material used in World War 2 fighter plane windows). She stood up in the middle of the surgery, got off the table and ran out of the theatre before I got to suture the wound. I was in the middle of the surgery!

"Hey, where are you going?" I shouted. "Arretez! Nous ne sommes pas finis!"(Stop we are not finished!) The nurse raised his voice and ran after the old lady who had already found her way out of the building.

This was a very distressing event. I had never heard of this happening to anyone else before. The next day the lady returned to the clinic. "She is in pain," I was told. As I carefully lifted her upper eyelid to view the surgical wound, I saw the intraocular lens had pushed the brown iris out of the wound. "Mon dieu, il faut le reparer toutes-suit."

That day, after I had repositioned the lens and iris back into their natural position, I sutured the wound with a thicker nylon suture than we use normally.

After three long weeks, having taken all the medication possible for tropical gastro enteritis that was available in the local pharmacy, I went back to Paris. First I had to drive a few hours through the savanna, take a little plane filled with tall African men in long white robes and that landed and took off on eight rural airstrips before finally arriving at the international airport in Yaounde. As soon as I arrived in Charles de Gaulle, the French International airport outside of Paris, I did a happy dance in the rain. I had been so hot and dehydrated and utterly sick while in Cameroon. My intestines would never really recuperate from the assault of tropical bacteria, worms, protozoa and strong medication I had to take for many months after.

I was still in severe abdominal pain weeks later and I got referred to the Institute Pasteur (named after the inventor of penicillin, the first antibiotic that would change humankind's life expectancy forever).

Professor Aron-Rosa asked me how many surgeries I had done. I told them. "Trente!" She took a step back. "Combien?"

I was embarrassed to admit I had done more than I was asked to do and stared at my shoes, like a puppy dog waiting for punishment. Looking back it doesn't seem like a lot but it was a few surgeries a day. They were shocked.

"And they let you do that?" she asked.

I pulled my shoulders up.

"Seems so." I looked up and smiled.

CHAPTER 11

I finally wake up

For my second year I finally got accepted in at the University of Antwerp and I moved back home, and straight back into the arms of Johan.

Johan and I were still together as a "steady couple" but The Eager Blonde was still ever-present in our lives and a growing pain in my ass. Johan still insisted that they were "just friends". We rented a two-bedroom apartment together in Wilrijk within a few steps of the hospital where I worked. We chose new furniture: a new modern white bedroom, a marble table in the dining room. My grandmother gave us a dishwasher as an engagement gift. I didn't see him every night as I was on call a lot. In the weekends we would stay at his parents' home and spend quality time with each other and our friends. But things were getting weirder. The blonde would hang out with us as part of the gang. She came on weekends away with Johan and me. They were great mates and seemed to be best friends in my eyes. Clearly she was into him. But he said he wasn't into her.

But things weren't right. I just didn't know what was going on. Was he dating her? Was he sleeping with her?

He told me no.

All the guys in our group told me no.

My instinct told me yes.

No, they all insisted. They are just good friends. Very good friends. So she became a part of our group in a way and I let her come along and join in all our fun.

There are two big hospitals in Antwerp and registrars can work or train at both of them. One was University Ziekenhuis Antwerpen (UZA) but I trained at Middelheim Ziekenhuis. It sits on the outskirts of Antwerp in the wealthy suburb of Wilrijk. It's a massive, modern tertiary university hospital with about 1 000 beds. The building is shaped like a plus sign with four wings and ten floors. Surgeries took place on the top floor, which had an amazing view over Antwerp.

I was a registrar, which was essentially a specialist surgeon in training. In Belgium the medical profession is segmented. As a Registrar you see and examine a patient, you advise the treatment and then you refer them to a more experienced consultant to do the actual surgery. In South Africa it was different. In South Africa the registrar or doctor did both the consultation and the surgery.

A registrar sees patients, orders tests,diagnoses conditions and treats patients. Registrars will refer patients to the consultant when they feel that their skill level is insufficient to deal with a particular patient's problem. A Registrar is a doctor who is less trained than a consultant but more trained than a house officer.

I worked on Ophthalmology Ward 6D. My job was to see the patients both before and after their surgery. I was a long way away from that young nurse who had sat on the deathbed of so many older people. I had moved into the medical field fully. My connection to the Angels had been long forgotten. Even my promise made that day in the sea felt like a distant dream.

But it was in Antwerp, the most unlikely of places, that the most unexpected person activated my promise.

The nurses' station in any hospital is the centre of each ward. That is where the doctors stop and get information about their patients or the family members gather and wait for news. There is always chatter and a cup of coffee to be had. It is the hub and the heart of each ward. I loved stopping in and chatting to the nurses. The medical field, and particularly ophthalmology, is a male-dominated profession in other countries but not in Belgium. Most ophthalmologists are female (90 percent) and so are most of the nurses.

Every day I would need their assistance in collecting all the eye patients from their beds and lining them up on a row of chairs next to the examination room. My job as a registrar entailed examining all admitted patients daily, before and after surgery. Middelheim Hospital had 1 000 beds and the eye ward had place for about 20 to30 patients.

I would arrive extra early so that all the work was done before any other doctors or colleagues arrived. I didn't like getting caught up in gossip or backstabbing. Unavoidably, in such a competitive group, it would happen that I created an enemy, usually through jealousy or just to push me off the throne of favourite registrar of the moment. It is part of life and I don't take it personally anymore, but my career and health has often suffered from the stress of being bullied by bosses or colleagues.

One day, while I was looking at a patient's chart, one of the nurses called Lieve walked up to the desk and sighed. She looked over my shoulder at the chart.

"That one is not going to last long because all the Angels are already in his room."
I froze. What did she just say? Angels?

This was the first medical person I had heard mention Angels. And here she was, openly talking about it as if it was common knowledge. What was more amazing was that all the other nurses at the station nodded as if in agreement.

I sat down with them and listened. I hung onto her every word. It was the first time I had met anyone, never mind a nurse, who saw Angels.

I joined the conversation and asked her what she meant.

The nurses told me that they knew when a patient was going to die soon as the spirits came to fetch them. "Spirits of deceased loved ones and Angels will gather in the room of very ill patients and wait for them to pass over," they told me.

Those few words confirmed my original view of the world. I was not the only one. I was not imagining it. There was something very special that happened in the rooms where people were dying. This was the first validation I had in my life that the things I felt, heard and saw were real.

I felt like I was floating. I was ecstatic. This was exciting. All the feelings came rushing back. All the years I had put that aside and focused on the medical side of things seemed to melt away. I remembered being that small girl with my hand held by an Angel walking down a dark street.

Why had I turned my back on that?

I knew that I had lost faith while attending the Catholic Convent school in my teenage years. It was almost two decades later and I was finding it again.

Lieve and I spoke for about an hour that day. For the next few days I kept seeking her out and chatting to her. It was a relationship that started that day but was to deepen over the years. I didn't know it then but she was about to become one of my best friends and a teacher to me in the ways of connecting deeper and deeper with these powers.

So that very casual comment on a seemingly normal day at work was the start of the change inside me. I was 27 and I suddenly realised that I had a power that was a real one. I could see and communicate with Angles and beings from another world. I also realised that I was not alone in this. I was not imaging it. I was not mad or delusional. It was real.

Years later she told me that I had also fascinated her from the start.

"You were easy going, friendly and you were also interested in spirituality and the alternative way of life, which was most interesting because I never experienced it before in the medical world. This was our common way of thinking, the start of our friendship. We both had a love of exploring the world in a way that is a little different from the common point of view. Friendship just happens, you don't question it!'"

For the first time in my life I wanted to learn how to use it. I dove deep into the world of esoteric exploration. It was about to change my life.

CHAPTER 12

A seeking journey begins

As Lieve drove her car up on the long, narrow driveway to the Tibetan Centre in the Chateau du Fond l'Eveque in Huy, I felt ready for a weekend of spiritual inquiry. I immediately felt at peace as we followed the long driveway through the green, leafy and lush oak trees. The energy of old trees always soothes my soul. Even as a small child, I would either lie supine on the grass or disappear to the local forest to declutter my mind and find my inner peace through connecting with nature.

The sea also calms me. But the closest sea was two hours drive away so I couldn't get there unless someone took me. But every year during my childhood my parents and I would spend a summer month at the Belgian seaside or sometimes at a lake in the Ardennes. I loved the water. I would kayak in my yellow rubber blow-up boat and go on daily pony rides.

Nature calls me in a powerful way. I am drawn to the green energy of plants and the cleansing energy of the water – the most healing to me is the salty seawater or crispy crystal clear running water in the mountain rivers of the Ardennes. I felt this calm coolness as we drove up to the castle that houses the Tibetan Centre.

Despite the many cars parked along the way towards the Tibetan Centre, it was quiet there and peace surrounded me. I immediately felt at home but also felt excited to learn more about these invisible but tangible energies.

The first time I went with Lieve to a Tibetan Ceremony For The Dead I didn't know what to expect but I trusted her as my spiritual teacher (and I never say no to an adventure either). What I found there changed me on a deep spiritual and cellular level forever.

I was introduced to the head of the centre, Lama Karpa, who didn't seem interested in me, but he professionally polite. Understandably he spoke instead to Lieve about the loss of her life partner.

The two of them had been studying a course of Powa for many years in order to pass on to the next chapter of life efficiently.

This is a ritual the Buddhist monks perform at the time of their death in order to guide their souls in the right direction. It used to be a secret ritual.

Lieve and her partner had to repeat a certain mantra 100 000 times before they were allowed to attend the Powa course.

They learned how to move their consciousness to a higher level, at the time of their own death and practised it several times in the Buddhist Centre in Huy.

I was to visit this centre many times over the next few years.

It was only one of many spiritual centres Lieve would take me to.

She was several years older than me but she shone with vitality. She was lean and healthy with short grey hair and wore glasses. She almost always wore comfortable (but not feminine) hiking sandals, even when it was cold. Her round glasses reminded me of John Lennon. She has the same birthday as me: the fourth of March. We are both spiritual souls. Pisces are often found in healing careers. At least three consultants and three other nurses I worked with were also Pisces. Statistically we Fish ruled that particular work environment.

Lieve introduced me to techniques such as visualisation of your dreams and Indian gurus like Sai Baba (she met him in person in his ashram in India). Together we went to blessing events with The Hugging Mother Amma; I had an audience with Mother Meera several times.

We once drove to a castle in Germany to see her. We had to wait outside in the cold and dark for ages. I was not impressed. We had booked in advance. You can have limited access to her. You don't pay. We were ushered into a room where we were told where to sit. We sat for an hour in silence. The Mother arrived in silence. One by one a row of people were told to go up to her throne and kneel in front of her. She put her hands on your head and downloaded this universal energy straight into you. Then she looked into your eyes and sent you a message.

What was so nice was that even as we drove to her, I got messages in my head. She was already talking to me. I asked her questions in my head. The last time I saw her was years later in Australia. I was dating a younger man and he was not right for me. I asked her if it was going to be okay. She said, "No, your relationship is not going to be okay, your exam is not going to be okay, but your kids are okay." She told me to get rid of my boyfriend as he was bad news.

Lieve gave me a picture of Sai Baba and Mother Meera and I used to carry them in my wallet for a long time. I would touch them when I needed healing energy.

One Friday Lieve and I went to a multi-cultural music festival that was a yearly event close to her home. She invited me to her cosy home, where she introduced me to her life partner. This lady, Lieve's soulmate and best friend, would die a few years later from breast cancer.

We went to spiritual fairs together where Lieve showed me where to find the best incense and taught me how to choose a crystal that speaks to you. That is a very individual choice, very much like selecting your kitten from a litter. It is a two-way street. The crystal that wants to work with you will draw your attention and then you have to hold it in your hand and feel the crystalline effect it has on your body.

Not all crystals feel good, especially if they have absorbed negative energy from the previous person that held them. Be very careful to only have cleared crystals around you.

CHAPTER 13

The beginning of the beginning

I had now been dating Johan for half my adult life and The Eager Blonde was going nowhere. When I had first heard about their relationship I had rationalised it by telling myself that he was lonely and needed someone. But he had totally denied they were sleeping together and had insisted they were just friends. For years!

When I had moved back I had fought for him. And I had won. We were back on track, living a seemingly contented life. But what I didn't know was that he had never ended the relationship he had started when I left Belgium.

I thought my entire life lay ahead of me, all planned and ready to roll. I was going to marry Johan and live and work as a specialist eye surgeon. That was how it was going to work out for me. Wasn't it? But something in me wasn't 100 percent sure. Not 100 Percent. I wasn't sure what that part was, and I am not sure I even acknowledged it.

At that stage Lieve had introduced me to an astrologer and suggested I should have a session.

Liliane sat me down and read my birth horoscope. She had prepared my birth horoscope based on where the planets were positioned at the exact time and place of my birth on the fourth of March 1968. My mother didn't remember what time I was born in the little town of Heist op den Berg.

"Your father had already left for work," was all she said. Men did not attend births, as it is customary these days. At least he wasn't getting drunk at the pub, hoping it would be a boy. My father was never ever drunk.

Liliane looked at me.

"You are going to have to leave your boyfriend and travel the world if you want to fulfil your destiny."

This statement was completely unexpected and startled me.

"Not possible. I am going to marry Johan; we are looking at houses to buy," I countered.

Liliane was not fazed.
"That is not gonna happen!" she told me. With certainty.

There were lots of opportunities in Belgium. My father wanted to buy me a mansion with an existing practice in it. But deep down I had an urge for adventure. Everyone wanted me to stay and I wanted to go. I could see myself stuck there for life, paying off a practice and doing the same thing day after day until I was old and grey.

Liliane saw I was a gypsy and that the conformist path ahead was wrong for me.

"South Africa is where your career and life will take off."

I was really upset and angry. This wasn't what I wanted to hear. I had come hoping for confirmation of my planned married life and instead she had turned it upside down. It messed up all my plans. I was shocked, angry and confused. And yet something she said spoke to my soul.

My intuitive self had already set up a connection in South Africa. In fact,during the year I would make a new friend in the form of one Professor Roux. The professor had come to Antwerp to do an advanced course in vitreoretinal surgery and had been observing live procedures at Middelheim Hospital.

People came from all over the world to study with Dr Zivojnovic who originated from Montenegro and was one of the top eye trauma specialists in the world. So we were lucky that we had specialist doctors from all over the world coming to study under him.

Earlier that year I had been chatting to a fellow registrar who was also in his last year of training, like me. He asked me where I wanted to be in a year's time and I said: "South Africa."

He had laughed.

"Well, if you want to go work in South Africa you'd better go upstairs. There is a South African professor watching the vitreoretinal surgery right now."

South Africa is a relative small country and it was unusual to find a South African surgeon in Antwerp! I dropped my work in the ward and rushed to the stairs. I charged straight up from the second to the tenth floor to the theatre section. I quickly changed into my surgical gown and went into the room where all the foreign visitors were watching the endoscopic surgery on a TV screen. I gathered my courage. Then I spoke up:

"Is there anyone from South Africa here?"
A man looked up.
"Ek is van Suid Africa" (I am from South Africa)," the friendly man with brown curly hair and thick old-fashioned glasses, answered, puzzled.

Everyone stared at me, as I was not supposed to be there. The viewing room was full of established VR surgeons from all over the world.

Destiny had brought us together here in this hospital in Antwerp where I was finishing my specialisation in Ophthalmology in a few months time.

He checked his diary.

"You are welcome to come and visit at Pretoria Academic Hospital. We have lots of Flemish students and doctors and you can start work in September."
My heart felt like jumping out of my chest and I wanted to kiss him .
"I'll be there."

So when the astrologer told me I was moving to South Africa it felt as if all the small links in a chain met in perfect alignment.

I was about to graduate that year after 11 years of studying to be a specialist ophthalmologist.

I was not going to stay and live in Belgium and marry Johan.
I was not going to compete with the blonde for the man I loved.
I was moving on.
I was moving to the other side of the equator.
I was going to leave him and leave my life.
I was going to follow the new path ahead of me.
And when I walked out of the session I was walking on air.

CHAPTER 14
I'm moving on

I tried to leave Johan at what he said was the worst possible time of his life. His father was dying of cancer.

He didn't want it to end. But I told him my plans. I told him that I was going to move to South Africa again. I told him I wasn't going to marry him. But he didn't want it to end. He said he loved me and the time was wrong. So I stayed a bit longer but I knew that he started up the relationship with The Eager Blonde yet again.

So I slowly drifted away from him over the next few months until there was nothing real of us left. It was hard for both of us. Johan's family was like a family to me. In fact, they were more of a family to me than mine had ever been. I loved them. I had spent most of my university years studying at their dining room table.

A year before I'd had a strange and unsettling conversation with Johan's dad. He'd sat me down one day.

"Veerle, I need a favour. It is a few years before I can retire but I am tired. I don't want to keep on working any more. Can you write me a letter saying that I am sick and I can't work anymore?"

I wasn't too surprised. This is not an unusual request if you are a doctor. You get all sorts of requests from friends to bail them out of problems.

I shook my head.

"No, sorry. You know I can't do that," I said.

He nodded.

'Then I need a promise. If I ever get a terminal disease can you please help me end my life? Can you please prescribe me some medication so I can die quickly?"

It was one of those moments where I felt a dreadful premonition come over me. My skin prickled and I felt the hair on my arms stand up.

I took it very seriously. I thought he knew something. I think subconsciously I knew it too. He had already had a deep vein thrombosis and this is often a sign of cancer (the malignant cells make the blood thicker).

So when he said this to me I got a real start. I felt something like recognition. But I put it aside.

I stroked his arm.
"If that ever happens to you we can talk at the time," I told him.

It wasn't even a year later that I was told he had developed terminal cancer. I had seen him a few times and I knew he was having chemotherapy.

I hadn't seen Johan for a while and he called out of the blue.

"Veerle, my dad wants to see you. Please come."
I dropped everything and went straight over.
He looked terrible and I sat by his bed for a long while.

He took my hand.
"You promised me you wouldn't let me suffer. I am not going to make it. This experimental chemotherapy is making me so sick. I don't want to go on anymore."

He described worrying cardiac symptoms and how he was feeling.

I suspected he was actually having a heart attack.
"You need to go to the hospital straight away!" I insisted. "This is not normal."
He shook his head.
"I refuse to be seen by students and junior doctors on call. The real specialists are not there on a Sunday."
"They will be consulted," I argued. "Your situation is too serious to stay at home. I will phone an ambulance."
"I forbid you to do that!" He squeezed my hand.
I went downstairs to where Johan and his mother were waiting.

"He needs to go to the emergency department at the hospital. This is serious, he needs urgent attention," I told them.

But the family said they had tried and tried. He didn't want to leave.

I shook my head.

"He is in a very bad condition. We need to call an ambulance now," I said.

As we were talking he appeared at the top of his stairs. He walked down the stairs, looking at all of us. Then he walked across the hall and collapsed into a chair and his heart stopped.

I rushed over. Johan and his mother were hysterical.

'Call an ambulance, NOW," I told them. I dragged his limp heavy body onto the floor. They called the ambulance and I continued to try and resuscitate him.

It seemed to go on forever and ever. I kept going and still no ambulance.

"Where is it! Call back," I said.

Johan called the dispatcher and found out that the ambulance had got lost.

At this stage I had been doing resuscitation for 30 minutes. But I noticed the dying man had brain damage. One pupil was big and the other small, a clear sign that he was brain dead.

I knew the signs. And I knew in my heart that it wasn't a coincidence that the ambulance got lost.

I remembered his wish a year ago.

I stopped pumping his heart. I knew he wanted to go. But Johan and his mom begged me to go on.

I asked them a few times if they were sure I should resuscitate him. Each time they said yes, yes, you must. Please do. Please.

I kept on but half-heartedly.

I knew it was over. I felt him pass on. I think it was the right way for him to go.

He died quickly, in his own home, surrounded by his loving family.

When the ambulance finally arrived I went out to meet them. I knew both the paramedics personally as we had grown up together in the same country town. I told them that the patient was already brain dead and had terminal pancreatic cancer. They reluctantly agreed to to resuscitate him and give him a shock with their defibrillator. But we all knew it was way too late.

Johan asked me to support him and walk behind his father's coffin next to him at the funeral, instead of his new official girlfriend. We had now broken up and she was his girlfriend. Finally it was real and final.

It is customary still to walk behind the coffin to the graveyard. I sat in the front of the church next to the family. The Eager Blonde sat at the back with the guests. It was confusing and uncomfortable for me. I reluctantly agreed to this charade for the sake of our decade-long friendship.

After the coffin reaches the graveyard you all gather, the casket gets lowered into the ground, the priest speaks and you throw some dirt on it. Johan and I were together in the front. We were the first to throw the dirt – together. Eager Blonde was far back in the queue. She walked past me, giving me evil looks.

After that the tradition is to go to a meeting hall and have coffee, tea, pastries and bread rolls with ham and cheese. Sometimes they also serve beer, which attracts more uninvited guests.

It was very tense. She was there. She was the girlfriend. All his friends were with her. I was hanging in, out of respect for his dad.

It went on and on. In winter it gets dark very early in Belgium. Around 6pm Johan and I left to drop his mother at home. At the time he was living at home to support her. Johan asked me to go for a ride on his BMW motorbike with him. We both wanted to drive off the heavy mood of the day and clear our heads.

His mother told us to dress up. She gave me a heavy-duty sailing jacket, which I pulled on. We both put on helmets. Johan put on his leather bike suit.

The air was freezing. There was no traffic. It was a Sunday evening.

The ground was hard. It was winter. The motorbike was powerful. The engine roared. He was angry. We had buried his father. We curved around the corner and I held on tight. He accelerated his bike. Two children suddenly ran out across the street pushing a go-cart.

The bike slipped sideways and we both flew off. We flew through the air. I watched sideways as the bike hit the third boy seated in the go-cart.

As I flew through the air it was as if time stood still. It froze from the second I lifted into the air to the second I hit the pavement.

The thoughts that went through my mind in this long period were logical: "I feel no fear. I am curious. Will this helmet protect my brain when I hit the concrete? I am suspended in mid-air. I feel Angels all around me. They are carrying me. I feel no fear. I know my Angels are protecting me."

When I was about 30 centimetres from the floor time sped up again and I fell. I hit my pelvis and the helmet bounced a few times, giving me a whiplash.

The helmet cracked, but not my head.

One of the boys was lying unconscious in the middle of the street.

A cyclist stopped. He was shouting at the kids and for their parents. The parents of the kids ran out from the house.

I got up quickly. I saw Johan lying on the ground. He scrambled up on one hand and I could see he had a broken collarbone. He stared at the child lying in the street. Johan was panicking, swinging his unbroken arm high into the air and screaming out loud: "No, no, no!" I got up and organised the emergency, calm as a doctor again.

I took control. I shouted at Johan to calm down. I checked the boy and saw there were no visible life-threatening injuries. He was still unconscious. I told the parents to call the ambulance. They wanted to move the boy but I insisted they didn't.

"He might have a fractured neck and moving him could kill him," I shouted. They didn't listen to me and lifted him up.

Finally the ambulance came.

The ambulance took off with the child and Johan went too.

I ask whether I could catch a ride in the front of the ambulance.

The boy had a fractured ankle and a mild concussion. They kept him overnight for observation. Again the parents wanted to take him home and we had a battle about that.

"When a trauma victim has been unconscious this means they have a concussion. They need to be observed for vital signs for 24 hours as they could get late brain swelling or an intracranial bleeding," I explained with calm authority.

After the boy had been attended to, we sat waiting in an emergency queue in Bonheiden Hospital – the closest hospital. Johan finally had an x-ray and it was confirmed he had a broken collarbone. I had x-rays of my spine and neck taken. The radiographer said it looked like there was a dislocated vertebra in my neck and called the doctor on call. The specialist told them he wasn't going to come and see me.

"It is late on a Sunday night," he said, "send her home." I suffered from typical whiplash symptoms for at least six weeks after that.

Later that night I looked back on the accident with wonder. I had not felt scared or worried at all. My feeling during the accident was just curiosity. I moved into doctor mode and took control and felt only that calm and peace of being in the zone, on purpose, doing what I was born to do.

Because Johan broke his collarbone he asked me to stay with him to care for him: to help him change his shirts and get dressed. I was finishing my last year as a registrar at Antwerp University and would leave for Pretoria in September 1997. I had an apartment with a view of my workplace, Middelheim Hospital.

But on the weekends I ended up having to stay with him and his mother.

I did that for a while but had to return to work and the relationship was over. For me it was clear that this was totally over. Johan had been my friend and lover for 13 years. It was hard to let go but my loyalty to him was wearing thin.

It sounds strange but the reality was that Johan and I were soul friends. We had been friends when we were teenagers before we started dating. And we actually remained friends once our love relationship ended. I could even say he was my best friend.

So it has hard to remove the entanglement of our friendship and our lives.

There was one more chapter of our relationship before it totally ended. And that played out during a trip a few months later to Mauritius.

It was a strange thing that even though we had split up and the Eager Blonde was his girlfriend, we still had one more exotic holiday planned together.

CHAPTER 15
Angels in flight

In the spring of 1997 Johan and his family and I had booked a weeklong holiday to Mauritius, a tropical island in the Indian Ocean, for my birthday. I have gifted myself a holiday every March since I turned 18. It was 1997. The holiday was booked and paid for.

His recently widowed mother and younger brother joined us, along with his brother's fiancé who was an old childhood friend of mine.

The group spent most of the days chilling next to the pool at the tropical resort. I was the action junkie as always and I spent most of my time underwater diving and snorkelling to find sea snakes, honeycomb eels and lionfish. A sea snake carries a deadly poison but its mouth is so small that it would need to aim for your little finger or ear in order to give you a lethal bite. I loved the way these dangerous creatures slithered through the crystal clear blue ocean.

Every sunset we met at the water's edge for drinks and dinner. I discovered the joy of Pina Coladas made with fresh coconut milk.

By the time we got on the British Airways flight back to London we were suntanned and relaxed. The smell of sun lotion and sea salt lingered on our happy bodies.

We took off, a heavy full big BA plane with over 500 passengers. Not long after takeoff we were told we were making an unscheduled landing in the Seychelles.

We were all asked to leave the plane. While we waited for the new passengers to check in, we sat in the little airport, the size of a one-room bungalow, without being offered any food or water. The heat was relentless at 40 degrees and we were outside with little shade. It took hours before we were told the plane had broken down and we had to wait for another plane to arrive from South Africa. After a tormenting, dehydrating eight hours it became clear no rescue plane was coming. The sweaty passengers were told to re-board the broken down plane for takeoff. It was a relief to escape the humid air. Once onboard, we sat without moving for at least another two hours. We were not offered any water. Finally we started moving and nerves were on edge as the plane gathered speed. At the last second the captain hit the brakes, bringing the plane to a shuddering halt just before the ocean's edge.

The runway is short on this island and the plane had been unable to get up the speed for lift off.

Why? It had just lost another engine.

We were all ushered out of the plane and back into the tiny airport terminal. There we were told that we would spend the night there. First class passengers were taken in a bus to a nearby hotel but the island was unable to accommodate more of us – so we were told. We were left in the airport terminal with no food and no drinks.

The holiday was over and this was turning into a nightmare. The smell of sun lotion had been replaced by a nervous, sweaty sweet odour. Suntans had turned into overheated and flushed skin. The relaxed holiday smiles had become tight lines of tension and stress as we waited hours and hours.

That night we were told the good news. A South African Airways plane was en route to collect us the next morning, as there were no spare parts on this little ex-French colony island in paradise. After a long and sleepless night we were finally are asked to board again. But it wasn't a South African Airways plane. It was the same British Airways boeing we had climbed off the day before. But we were now a group of survivors who just wanted to get home. So the hot, stinky full plane of grumpy passengers taxied up the runway for take off again. I could see the ocean approaching through my little window and felt a mix of fear and relief. Finally.

SLAM! We hit the brakes again! It was our second unsuccessful departure.

Now the story becomes really unbelievable. The plane taxied back to the airport terminal, which was basically a shed the size of a triple garage. But this time the poor hot thirsty passengers were not even offloaded. And there we sat for a full hour.

Then the co-pilot made the following intercom announcement

"Ladies and gentlemen, I am sorry to inform you that during our last takeoff a second engine broke. London has calculated that we are still able to take off like this, with only two engines working. But we have had to offload all the extra kerosene and baggage. Ladies and gentlemen I assure you that I have family on this plane and I wouldn't risk this if it weren't totally safe. So please relax and we will take off soon."

Now I believe in the rule of threes. I don't like threes. A third attempt at takeoff? I was not willing to bet my life on it. I jumped out of my seat and walked up the steward.

"I want to get off this plane!"

"That would mean you have to wait for the next flight in a week's time and all the hotels are full," he replied.

"I don't care whether I have to sleep on the beach for a week! I want to live so I want to get off this plane NOW!"

The steward spoke to the pilot over the indoor communication system and then answered.

"You are not to leave this plane as this would mean offloading all the luggage to search for your suitcase, and we can't be delayed any longer."

I was mad. After ten hours of heat and no water I was ready to fight. I stood strong and straight, shoulders back, fiery blue eyes piercing…. My fists were tight balls and I was ready to pounce for the handle that unlocks the airplane door.

The steward, however, was clearly experienced and not fazed by the hysterical female passenger. He grabbed me by my arm and threatened to have me arrested for dangerous behaviour. Then he marched me back to my seat.

"Keep her calm, will you?" he demanded my embarrassed boyfriend and his mother.

They gave me The Look.

"Bad, bad girl, conform like all other passengers on the plane of death!" I read in their eyes.

I had no choice at all. I could feel the fear rising in me like thick, dark water. We were all going to die.

The atmosphere in the plane was tangible. Apart from me, the crazy Belgian doctor, all the others were good sheep on their way to the slaughterhouse: silent, big pupils, head down, defeated and frozen by fear. The smell of fear filled the cattle class. I am pretty sure it filled first class too!

If I had had a sharp object I could have sliced the tension in pieces like a cake; that is how dense and low the negative energy of fear is when it accumulates. I could feel it dragging me in. I knew I needed to escape it.

That is when I decided to leave my body. I wanted to leave before the gruesome experience of crashing and burning in the plane. So I sat down. I put myself in yoga position, legs crossed, eyes closed. I put my hands in a mudra position (thumbs touching second and third fingertips, like a closed lotus flower). Then I did something I haven't done since childhood. I called for my Angels to come and get me.

Even though I hadn't called on them for almost a decade since the near-drowning incident in South Africa they arrived in a heartbeat.

"Please, come get me now, Angels," I cried out inside my head aiming for the heavens. "I don't want to be present when this plane crashes and burns. "I don't want to see hundreds of people in such fear and pain. Come take me now, please."

My Angels collected my spirit and swept me up into the heavens with them. I felt myself leave my body in yoga position in the Boeing. I felt safe and protected in my Angels' hands as they took me far above the group on a journey to a safe place.

I was back in the feeling I had almost forgotten. I felt like I was flying, seeing places from a bird's perspective as the gentle touch of my Angels held my hands. We flashed through the stars and universes in seconds.

Back down where my body was sitting on the Boeing I was aware that the plane was in the air and that the seatbelt light had been turned off.

Visiting those heavenly places is so magical and peaceful. Time stands still. Beauty and love and expansion are all around. And I had almost forgotten about it. I had forgotten how close my Angels were to me, and that I could call them. I was rolling in the love of the memory.

No wonder I wasn't keen to return to the heavy earth energy surrounded by the stench of fear and low vibration. But I came back and I endured the rest of the ten-hour flight. I was calm and centred.

At that stage we finally got a glass of water. One glass each only for the duration of a ten hour flight as they had offloaded all food and beverage supplies for economy passengers to make the plane lighter.

But something had changed for me on that flight. I hadn't yet put all the pieces into place but I know that day I remembered my connection to my Angels. How could I have forgotten them for so long? I had experienced hints of them in the wards while caring for the terminally ill. But most often those were the deceased loved ones waiting for the dying to return home with them and their Guardian Angels. They were looser things, feelings of energy. But these Angels who came for me … I knew them. I remembered them in a way that was tangible and real.

Slowly the small girl standing alone on the abandoned street, the one who found an Angel to walk her home at night, was finding her way back.

CHAPTER 16

Fate answers

Despite all the turmoil at home, when the day came to get on the plane to South Africa, nothing was going to stop me.

I answered the call with a big smile on my face. I was sure I could hear my Angels and guides doing a happy dance. I was going exactly where I was supposed to be in order to start the best part of my life in my favourite country: South Africa.

How easy was that? No need to send 100 application letters. The deal was done in the theatre that day with Professor Roux. We shook hands and smiled.

He trusted me and gave me amazing opportunities to excel in my developing career as a vitreoretinal surgeon on eyes that were traumatised by violence - guns and bomb explosions - or in a far advanced stage of diabetes or scarred from long-standing retinal detachments.

My bosses in Antwerp had pioneered a lot of surgical techniques and instruments for vitreoretinal surgery. I took that knowledge to South Africa and Australia. Some of the techniques I shared there are still used today.

I also did a prospective three-year study on patients with retinal detachments that got hailed all over the world amongst retinal surgeons. It is because of having observed their genius in desperate cases that I also wanted to become a vitreoretinal surgeon. It is the top of advanced technology to peel micron thin membranes off a retina with microscopically small titanium forceps and scissors, while visualising the retina through the microscope, cornea and lens.

I was so ready for a clean, new start when I got on the plane to Johannesburg. I had a feeling of unavoidable destiny.

I had been exchanging emails with Professor Polla Roux for months and we had fixed my terms. I agreed to come for six months. But I was not going to get paid and the trip was on my own account. After years of study my finances were depleted. So my father sponsored me after a difficult conversation.

"Are you sure you want to waste all your study effort to work for free in Africa?" my father asked me earnestly.

He had the mind of an accountant and all his sacrifices to help me through medical school were not giving him the immediate profit he had expected. "I know I have to do this for my career … and for my thirst for adventure and exploration," I added when that argument only partially convinced him.

"And for a date orchestrated in heaven with my still unknown next soulmate," my spirit added from the other realm.

I had to pay for the flight and I knew from having lived there I would have to buy an old car. You need a car in South Africa to get around. Public transport and the streets are not safe. I decided to start my life there attending a professional conference at a hotel and casino resort called Sun City.

I had booked a shared room in The Palace, my favourite luxurious hotel in the resort. It was beautifully placed in a green valley surrounded by sandy sunny hills. As our transport drove up the long drive, the sand coloured African-style Palace was reflecting the bright sun rays. Outside the impressive entrance stands a large fountain circled by four golden gemsbok. The lobby is as big and ornate as a dance hall. The beautiful marble mosaic floors glisten and feel cool and polished. The zebra skin throne referred to the African Kingdoms. There are huge halls, atriums, waterfalls and pools to enjoy. The walk down the big steps towards the Valley of Thunder has an ancient design with a temple, an atrium and a swinging hang bridge through the jungle. I really like this place that oozes adventure in a stylish way.

I had a Belgian girlfriend who was an ophthalmology registrar who was travelling with her parents and siblings to have an African safari experience. She was also attending the conference so we shared a room at the Palace of the Lost City. That was my start in South Africa. It was the best place to meet everyone in my field. I made friends with the liberal Capetonians easily. They were also retinal specialists. We would meet up at all the specialty conferences for the next six years. The first day we clicked and we danced the night away in the disco. My future colleagues from Pretoria were more conservative and had no time for me but that didn't worry me. I was new in the field and I wanted to learn all I could. In evenings we socialised and partied. I met three nice South Africa ophthalmologists from Cape Town. We went dancing at night instead of gambling at the casino tables. The energy in casinos is so terribly low and dense and I avoid those places like the plague. We had so much fun together. They were a few years older than me but where I wanted to be and I felt like I had already found some people I could relate to on my first few days. They were all to become good friends of mine.

After the surreal glamour of Sun City I headed back to the grim reality of Pretoria to Kalafong Hospital where I was to be stationed. Kalafong Hospital is a public hospital on the western outskirts of Pretoria in the suburb of Atteridgeville and serves a mostly black population. Because of this its funding was dire. In those days it was one of the worst funded hospitals and decades on little has changed.

The hospital was like working in a remote outpost with old, malfunctioning equipment. There was bad or little equipment. Some days the linen truck was hijacked and I was not allowed to operate. Other days the porters were on strike. Many days there was no clean linen or the instruments hadn't been cleaned. It was like working in the Wild West.

While I was based at Kalafong I reported to the bigger Pretoria Academic Hospital. I rented a granny flat in Waterfkloof. It was in a house of a lady whose brother was one of my colleagues in training.

It was a bit lonely. I had no real friends but received faxes full of poetry from a romantic Latino boyfriend I left behind in Belgium.

I also enjoyed keeping up. The hospital doctors were pretty busy and it was clearly a boys club. I didn't make myself popular either. On the first day I followed the boys to lunch. They were playing table tennis and silly me.... I beat them all!! That was a big mistake.

Later on I was told: "It is too humiliating for a man to be taught anything by a woman!"

It was an introduction to South African men. Welcome to the boy's club. They were younger guys. My equals. But they saw me as big competition. I have always been competitive. In South Africa medicine is a male dominated profession. It is number one on the list of desirable medical specialties.

The system in South Africa was confusing and less organised than Europe. A lot of the time the nurses overruled me. I was angry a lot of the time. It was so unfair. But the nurses were the bosses and they controlled the surgery, the clinic, the appointments and everything else. This is common in Commonwealth countries and particular in public hospitals. Even with administrative staff. There were no consultants to guide the registrars at Kalafong Hospital at all. We just had to survive and figure it out.

It was very hard for patients to get there and sometimes they travelled for three days (and had to take a loan to get there) while they could hardly see because of cataracts.

My professor took a sabbatical leave to do a large population study on glaucoma. A young Jewish female who came from Johannesburg replaced him. She was brilliant. She was amazed that I had worked for a year and they had not paid me. She looked into it and found that private male doctors who were getting paid for consultant work had never showed up.

She asked me to call them and ask if they would agree to reallocate that budget to create a position for me. They all agreed!

So she reallocated the budget and I got a half-time salary. It was enough to survive.

I had also asked if I could do housesitting and one of the ophthalmologists offered me his granny flat. I moved in with a wonderful family - Harold and Bibi (a GP) and their children. It was the best time of my life. They loved each other and were nice to each other and I just blended in. Until that moment I had never known that families could be warm and loving. My experience of a family was a group of people who ignore each other or shout at each other. This was my first experience of a happy family. Their welcoming kindness changed me forever. Until then I had decided that I would never have children of my own but now family had taken on a new meaning.

CHAPTER 17

Angels in human form

Sister Meir, the nurse who ruled the ophthalmic theatre in Pretoria Academic Hospital, was a sweet but fiery old sister who ruled with an iron fist. She was helped by an intelligent and efficient, charming young blonde assistant, who flirted herself into the hearts of the male doctors (and into a few beds too).

Sister Meir often assisted during surgery. She fascinated me because every time we prepared for surgery she would pray. She would do it openly and so everyone could hear. This was all new to me. But to her it was natural.

I watched her praying each time. She said she prayed quietly before every operation but sometimes when things weren't going well she would speak out loud and call for help.

When machines wouldn't work, she would call out with a sigh: "*O Here, help ons*" which is Afrikaans for "Oh Lord, help us".

And lo and behold the cataract removal (phaco) machine would stutter back to life, the lights would come back on, the oxygen supply started flowing again. It was uncanny.

She would say things like "*Die Here* (God) come down and help us here. We need you now. Make this operation go smoothly. Make this machine work."

They were simple and honest things. I was fascinated.

When she tuned in and prayed things felt better. I started to ask her to pray for me too. If I could see things weren't going well in a surgery I would nod to her. Prayer time.

She would pray, no questions asked. And most often things turned around. When you are in a higher vibration of connecting with God you don't have fear and you go straight to the source. Help can flow. Fear is a low vibration.

This was the first time I had met someone who was deeply religious but openly so.

In fact most of the Afrikaans people seemed to have that easy, light way with religion.

Religion seems to be on the surface of their lives. Many have a constant feeling of God with them. I was drawn to that and felt that welcoming and loving feeling that comes from an open heart. Even with the racial tension still lingering after the end of apartheid I saw the South African people as being very loving, giving, caring and kind. It was the first time the presence of God was felt in every day.

The people felt to me as if they came from the heart. It was another world from cold Belgium where people are so spoiled that they complain about the small stuff. Very few have remained religious and with most Belgians there is no connection to God or spirit. In South Africa I was constantly surrounded by a high vibrational energy of love and gratitude, even at work.

I started being grateful for being alive when I woke up in the morning (gunshots that killed the neighbours and the searching police helicopters reminded me every night how fragile my life really was). I felt like I had finally found my true home.

I had lost faith attending the Catholic convent school in my teenage years and it felt like I was finding it again. I started a deep belief in God and his helpers in South Africa.

It is a land of sharp contrasts, between dark and white skin and intentions, hot and cold climates, deep seas and high mountains: it is truly a magnificent place. I suspect God had a field day creating this colourful place, where I feel most at home, an outpost of unbridled creativity.

I now had a paid job and my life started to settle and take on a more familiar rhythm.

I had made a few friends. My landlord had a brother who was nice enough to introduce me to a group of scuba divers with whom I would go on fantastic dive holidays. Roughing it under the palm trees on a Mozambican beach, jumping on a whale shark the size of a submarine, dropping out of a dingy circled by adult white pointed reef sharks.

"What do we do now?" I asked the dive master glaring at the large predators surrounding us in our tiny boat. "Drop down fast," she answered just before she put on her mask and mouthpiece in place. She fell tank-first backwards in the waves and disappeared out of sight into the deep blue. "I don't want to stay here alone with 10 sharks," I decided, and followed the rest of the group to the bottom of the sea.

I made a new friend who was an admin staff member for an organisation offering free clinics and cataract surgery in the outback. I volunteered much of my free time driving into the unknown on dirt roads. Operating on 20 cataracts a day was a normal day. It was tiring, as this was done the manual (extra capsular), not the modern (phaco emulsification) way. We travelled through the Namibian desert and along Skeleton coast in his little Volkswagen.

I was 28 and I was content and busy. I was learning and doing interesting things. I even saw the environment as challenging and new. I became used to bad and old equipment – I even got electrocuted once using some old pieces. I was on a rolling chair and I got thrown five metres backwards on the wheels. But it was an adventure. There were African challenges to deal with. No common language! Nurses on strike on Friday!

It was crazy!

CHAPTER 18
Astral traveling

But something had been sparked in me that was growing every day. It was a growing need to find a deeper connection to spirituality. Sister Meir who so openly called to God sparked part of this.

I had felt this calling inside of me for a while now. I just wasn't sure how to find it.

My first clue came during a visit to my favourite bookstore in Waterkloof. I walked one day into Exclusive Books and walked straight to a shelf. My fingers ran along the spines and I picked up a book that drew me. It was on astral travelling and remote viewing, written by an ex-military person who had taught this technique for espionage in the US army. I bought it immediately and devoured it in a few hours.

And it was only then, as an adult, that I remembered my nightly trips.

I knew that! I remembered!

It was all coming back to me. All the connections I had as a child that I had shoved somewhere far away during my years at the convent school. They were coming back to me.

There were some exercises that I tried and voila!

But I didn't do this all the time. I was interested, but not obsessed. I started to out-of-body travel more. After all, I had a good amount of free time as a single lady.

Astral travelling feels like the most natural thing in the world to me. Many times people ask me how I do it. But the process was always so seamless and natural that it is hard to break down the experience. It started as flying with Angels as a child. It was like they were taking my hand and we were going on a trip. On one level it feels as if my spirit leaves my body. I can travel at the speed of light. I just asked my Angels to take me somewhere and it happened.

I did it without ever reading a book about it. It was only years later that I put a name to it.

This is very different to dreaming. You actually leave your body and you can float over it and see it.

As a little child, my parents always put me to bed way too early around 5pm in the evening and told me not to come out of my room. They wanted to get rid of me so they could watch TV. I was not tired and I was bored. I used to think: "Where should I go today?" I would think of where I wanted to fly – see Africa, visit a friend, and see the sun. I may have heard the words but I didn't actually know where Africa was. I had a vague idea because of the Tintin stories my father read to me. I would close my eyes and just will it to happen.

My body would relax in a very deep way and in seconds I would flash out of my human vessel.

Sometimes I would hang around in my bedroom for a bit. When I started I would explore the town, the streets and friend's houses. But I started to go further and further. As I got braver I could move to places in a flash.

I met people along the way. They were not real people but beings on the soul plane. It felt so familiar. I just wanted to hug them and stay with them, but I am not sure who they are in real life.

As I fall asleep, I would think: "I want to be there" and I would arrive there in flash. I can travel anywhere on our planet or others. The same process is repeated when I want to return to my body. I simply think it and I am there. I am back and everything is normal. The room is around me and I see everything.

While I am travelling I look as if I am asleep. If someone could see my body I would look asleep but I am very conscious. If someone spoke to me I would eventually hear him or her, return to my body and wake up slowly. Returning to my body usually happens in an instant. Sometimes I could not get back into my human vessel and that seriously freaked me out.

I also left the planet and went into space. I never landed on a planet or the moon! But I would just fly into the universe and there was the most enormous sense of freedom.

My astral travels took about an hour or two. Whenever I felt I had enough, I just came back. Sometimes I would have to return. If someone came into my room and spoke to me, I would zip back into my body and wake up painfully. Other times it was a choice to return. If I got sleepy I often knew it was time to go home. But I was always awake. It was almost like a bit of a jolt when I returned to my body. Most times it was dark and I was ready to go to sleep.

So what leaves and what stays? Well, your physical body stays behind. I wonder: the part of me that astral travels, is it my energy/ consciousness and is that the same as my soul and higher self? My mind was in control. I recall being very conscious and in control. So at one level it was my consciousness. I had no idea of what was happening to my body at all.

One problem I have found is that once my soul leaves, the body is an empty shell and at that time it can be invaded by other beings. As a child I didn't think of any dangers. And luckily none appeared.

The first times I astral travelled, it was like a waking dream.

As a child I wouldn't really plan where I would go next but I would have a general idea of where I wanted to travel to next.

Later on, in adult life, I saw a map of the world with places where different soul friends of mine live on this earthly plane so I started to make a conscious choice of where I wanted to go.

I was a bit lonely in my single flat in Pretoria. I didn't have that many friends really so every night I would connect with these soul friends on the astral plane. This was my strange social life!

So what were these friends like? It was like a feeling of knowing someone. Here you are! I never saw form. It was more of an energy. There was no body to look at. Remember that I had left my own body so I didn't have a form either. I don't honestly know if they were dead or alive. I don't even know if they were the same people or different people.

I tried looking at them, asking names, I asked: "How can I find you? Where do you live? Can I find you in real life?" But nothing!

Once I decided to go search for my future friends and I had a cat and a dog show up. The black cat had white feet and one blue and one brown eye. The cat spoke to me.

"Don't worry I will be your friend."

The border collie (with a blue and brown eye) said, "And I will protect you". The next day I went to a pet shop in Pretoria and there was the cat. The kitten clung onto me and didn't want to let go. He knew he belonged with me. I took him home straight away. On the way home in the car he sat on my head and shoulders. He wanted to see where he was going to live for the next year. My friendly soul cat would travel up and down between Africa and Europe with us a few times. He also kept my son Matthew company in his cradle from day one. When we moved to Australia Poquito became my mum's best friend and companion. Currently he is enjoying retirement with my Belgian godfather.

My life became very clear and focused. I worked hard for long hours. I exercised in the gym every day. I meditated every night.

On the days that I finished work early, I went to Exclusive Books. I could sit there for hours on a soft leather couch, with a coffee and get lost in books. I wasn't aware that I was trying to gather knowledge.

As I discovered more and more about the spiritual world through reading and experimenting at home, the influence stuck with me during my day job in the hospital. I managed to see an enormous amount of patients a day in the clinic. Fifty a day was not an exception and these were patients who most of the time didn't speak either English or Afrikaans. Sometimes a nurse translated for me but that was not always correct either. I used an enormous amount of intuition to diagnose these patients correctly without any form of communication. I used Clair knowing – a form of clairvoyance where you simply just know.

It was the same during surgery: I couldn't communicate with the patient so I felt what they were feeling. That is called Clair sentient and so I could anticipate problems. Their Guardian Angels were no doubt whispering advice in my ears and my guides were instructing me on how to avoid complications and get the best outcome. They walked from my nightly travels into my work life and have never left. Angels only speak up when you ask though. Spirit guides show up when they want to. You always have free will. You can choose not to ask for help from above and to learn slowly from your mistakes. After all we are humans, not gods.

CHAPTER 19
Meeting a soul mate

I had been living in Pretoria for two years when I met the man I was to marry. I was flying to the coastal town of Knysna, alone, for a conference. As I walked onto the plane, I looked at my ticket. There was a man sitting in the seat next to me.

I was the last one to board, in a hurry, all flustered, and he was sitting there. A slight blonde man with thick strawberry blonde hair. He was not a big man. Around 1.75m. He was lean and well proportioned. Bright blue eyes and blonde eyelashes. Even the hair on his arm was blonde.

He had crooked teeth and a long neck with a tan. He was cleanly shaven. He wasn't particularly my type.

He wore tartan print shirts with short sleeves and beige cotton chinos or jeans. In my opinion he looked a bit old fashioned but he thought it was proper. He was proper and decent and clean. A bit boring for me.

But as soon I saw him I just knew I was going to be with him.

I remember thinking… oh no, not now. I don't want to meet The Guy now. I wasn't ready to meet him. I was crazy about another guy but he wasn't into me. I was feeling rejected and down. I wasn't in the mood to meet anyone. I just wanted to read my book, How to Get What You Want and Want What You Have by John Gray.

I recognised him as mine. I just didn't think the timing was right. But he did! He was super friendly and polite and wanted to talk.

I largely ignored him during the flight but he kept trying to talk to me anyway. I wanted to read my book. I was very intrigued by its content and I filled in the manifesting checklist of the perfect partner. So for much of the trip I gave him the cold shoulder. He eventually got my attention though, by talking about scuba diving destinations. Both of us wanted to go on a dive safari to Madagascar and to the Maldives. We had found ourselves a travel buddy!

He offered me a ride from the airport but I was getting a lift with colleagues so I said no. Later that day I went to the beach with my book. I finished filling in the checklist for my soulmate. I didn't know that Mark had come to the hotel to find me. He left a note under my door asking me for dinner that night with all his friends. I didn't want to go but later that day I bumped into him. He was back at my hotel to find me! He asked me out again.

All right then! I agreed to dinner. We had oyster and delicious white wine. His friends were nice people and we all had a good laugh. I found out he was an architect and lived relatively close to me, in Johannesburg.

I was having a blast but after dinner I started to feel sick. It got worse and worse but of course I still continued to have fun. We left late to drive back to the hotel. "I feel dreadful, "" I uttered. I was going to be sick. "Pull over!" I yelled. He stopped and I ran out of the car behind a bush where I threw up. I am sure it was a bad oyster. I was crouching behind the bush when I realised I was not just going to be sick. It was going to come out both ends! Oh, this was embarrassing. Worse! He followed me. He found me on our first date butt naked behind a bush. He always joked about it and never let me live that one down.

That was our first date!

When I went back to Pretoria the relationship just continued effortlessly. Mark lived and worked in Johannesburg and every weekend we saw each other. Mark's clothes may have been a bit old fashioned but he loved adventure. We had so many things in common. We both loved scuba diving and he was looking for a dive partner and so was I. He put such an effort into making everything we did special. He took me to the best places and swept me off my feet. They were perfect for me. They were unusual experiences and that was so right for me.

He took me to so many magical places. He took me to the Lion Park to cuddle four lion cubs and to the Rosebank Mall Craft Market on Sundays.

He took me to theatre and shows. We went to watch Pieter Dirk Uys /Evita, the South African comedian. I belly laughed till tears were running down my cheeks. That night, after a hot meal at a Thai restaurant, Mark won me over with the most colourful bouquet of tulips. He scored again with all the trips he took me on. I loved adventure! Shark diving, scuba diving. We did something exciting every weekend. We went hiking in the hills and mountains.

Every night now I had dinner or drinks with friends. I had the most wonderful time in Africa from the moment I met him.

He told me that when he had looked at my blue eyes that first time he knew that I was the one he wanted to spend his life with. He tried and kept trying. He chased me and he finally got me.

I got to know his family. Mark's mum is a gracious elderly lady resembling the Queen of England. She was very kind, funny and religious. She had become a widow in her forties. Left with two little boys, she had resumed work as a secretary and had never remarried. Another family member later told me that a curse had been put on all the second Wightman sons in Scotland somewhere. They all die from cancer at the same young age and leave behind young children. Everybody loves Maureen, just like everybody liked Mark Wightman.

Mark's talent was being the second in command. He thrived on working for great architects and he thrived running our house. He never wanted to take over the prime position, and seemingly never felt resentful of my career or my drive. He did all the washing and the dishes. His place was sparkly clean (he was a bit compulsive).

I had such a happy life. I lived with a family. I had a wonderful boyfriend. I was doing amazing healing work and I felt grateful and connected. This was the best time of my life!

Even though the second I had met him I had the uncanny feeling that he was my soulmate, life moved on and I forgot that feeling and dove into the relationship. But months later I found a drawing that reminded me that our meeting was fate. I had done the drawing on the same day I met him on the plane to Knysna.

It was an exercise from the book I was reading: How to get What You Want and Want What You Have. You had to draw what you wanted. On the beach later that day I made a drawing of a man giving me a bunch of tulips. On paper I was wearing a blouse with flaring sleeves I didn't own at that stage but would wear on our first date night. I wrote a list of what I wanted in the man who was to share my life.

It was months later before this was to happen. It happened on the first night we had sex. We had been dating for two months when I finally stayed the night with him in Johannesburg. He took me to the theatre and then to dinner at a Thai restaurant in Rosebank. We stayed at a friend's house that had lots of rooms. There was a big bed and as I walked into the room there was a vase of ten tulips. They were mixed red, black and yellow. They were the flowers from my drawing.

Later I found the drawing in the John Gray book and as I looked at it I knew that I had manifested Mark to show up in my life. He was right there all along in the drawing.

I know then that our meeting was the signal the two of us had organised before we were born. I believe we make these soul deals. It had been the same with my first love, Johan.

CHAPTER 20
Working with my energy

Soon after I met Mark we went to Madagascar for a week of scuba diving from a catamaran. On the plane home we sat in the first row. During the flight I left my body. I wasn't aware of why I did this. I don't remember leaving but the first thing I knew was that I couldn't get back into my body.

It felt as if my body was moving faster than my soul. I felt this empty body sitting in a chair and there was me as an energy blob with strands hanging off it struggling to connect. I had a visual image of it that I can never erase. It was like I was in watercolour and I was running out. It seemed like the plane was moving too fast for my energy body to catch up. It was the first time I had a problem with this natural ability. At a speed of 1 000 kilometres an hour, I struggled to catch up. I panicked. I don't recall what I did but then in a zap I was back inside. For the first time I had been scared.

I felt a bit unwell for a bit after that but slowly I came back to normal. This took more than a few hours, more like a few weeks. I felt as if a part of me had not returned and was lost somewhere. I felt ungrounded and as thin as a waft of smoke for a while.

I was freaked out. Luckily I spoke to a few friends and they gave me advice about what to do.

There have been times when I have been scared. I was back from South Africa on a visit to Belgium and I was at home visiting my parents. I was sleeping in my old bedroom. I was a more experienced astral traveller by then. I had been reading books about it and I was practicing. I had been on a journey and I felt it was time to go home. I wanted to wake up and end it. I returned to the room but I could not get inside my own body. There I saw my empty shell.

I saw a black entity inside my body and felt as if my body had been taken by other beings. I remember a teacher telling me tolook yourself in your eyes if you can't get in. I tried that and it didn't work. I got so angry – I was screaming at them: "GET OUT! This is MY BODY!"

My energy body was holding my own arms and trying to get in somewhere at the back of the head. But my body was asleep and didn't wake up. As soon as I said the words I was back in my body.

There were times that my travels were deeper and took me into different places. There was a time that I took off work and focused on healing. I was working consciously with finding solutions. At this time I was doing guided meditations that connected with different energies. During this time I visited strange places.

I recall a time that I was travelling in the astral plane and I saw familiar souls, spread all over the planet, like beacons of light. I knew they were my soulmates and they were living all over the world, dotted around. "Mmm," I thought, excited, "there they are! I wonder if I will meet them all?"

The astral plane does not have a high level of consciousness; it exists on the human level. The Angels can visit all levels of existence, without any effort. I work with Angels in a variety of planes.

Some of the energies I met were higher beings. This was not during astral travelling but during a guided meditation. The beings I met were light beings – and the closest I can compare them to are the mythical Greek gods on thrones next to each other. This was the highest plane I have ever been on. It felt as if I was before St Peter's Gate, for those who are religious. I call it the Plane of Thrones. These beings were not really Greek gods but energetic beings of very high energy in the cosmic sense. I was taken to a half circle of thrones with beings. The feeling was onerous, of judgment and weighing up my life. They were sitting there, all these men with long beards and they were going to weigh up my life and choices and judge me. They were calling on me to judge my life and myself. I got to sit on one of the middle thrones. They were looking at me. I asked what I needed to learn in this lifetime. They told me to look to my left. I think it was my dark side. It scared me enormously and I jumped back into my body. I was too scared to look because I could feel Darkness. As I started to feel the scary energy I flashed out. I came back.

CHAPTER 21

The flying years

I went from working with no salary for a year to getting a paid job as a medical officer. Then I got a registrar position and I passed the South African College exams in 2000. I became a Fellow of the South African College and I continued my work as a vitreoretinal specialist and consultant. I had learned so much from being exposed to challenging surgery in extreme cases, in difficult conditions, for a full four years.

For all this time Mark was my entire life and my total support system. We were a wonderful couple. It was a dream relationship in all ways. We were a great match – emotionally, physically, sexually, spiritually, verbally....

It was an adventure. It was the best time of my life.

I visited Belgium twice a year to do advanced courses. But then an offer came to start my own department in Belgium.

We were sitting in a restaurant when I told him about the offer. Mark stared at me, his face shocked. Then his eyes welled up and he cried. This was an unexpected reaction!

"You can't leave me!" he said. "I can't live without you."

I was so relieved when I realised what was wrong.

But I had really wanted him to tell me not to go. He was ecstatic. He wanted to leave South Africa. He wanted to travel to Europe and he was thrilled.

I told him he could come. Of course I had expected him to come.

Everyone encouraged me and said it all sounded great. People told me it was a great opportunity, an amazing career move and that I was lucky. And on paper all of this was true. But to tell the truth, I didn't want the job. I loved my life in South Africa. But Mark really wanted to go. So I gave my potential future colleagues and hospital lots of outrageous demands. I asked for the newest and most expensive equipment on offer and a substantial salary. I asked for lots of impossible things.

They said yes to all my demands. We moved to Belgium in 2001. We packed up our life, said farewell to our friends and Mark's family. We both said goodbye to our jobs and moved our entire lives to Bruges to make a new start.

We settled easily into a relaxed and successful life in Bruges. Mark got a job at my hospital. They were doing major renovations and he worked as an architect on the job. He was always easy going and popular. He wasn't like me. I was confrontational, forthright and challenging. I was ambitious and wanted to be a great surgeon. He was happy to support me and run the house. We made a great pair.

Mark started Flemish language classes and fitted in really fast. When we first arrived in Belgium we had slept in a friend's tiny seaside studio but soon we found a beautiful house that wasvery modern and light. We had nothing when we moved in but we quickly bought furniture. Mark did all the interior decoration with a lot of love and attention to detail. The house was in a suburb called St Michiels next to a big forest with an old castle in it. If you walked out of our house and turned left you would find a Michelin star restaurant, and if you turned right you'd walk into the forest. The castle was surrounded by a moat and black swans. We often put on warm coats, jumped in the car and went for a walk on the North Sea beaches in winter. In summer we would lie on the beach and read.

The change for me was not just moving from one country to another – it was also moving from a government hospital to a semi- private practice. The difference was the money. The money in a semi-private hospital is a great deal more than what you earn while working for a government or academic hospital. In Belgium patients get virtually all their health costs covered by the government, no matter which doctor or hospital they choose to go to.

I was one of only ten retinal surgeons in the entire country and suddenly I was a celebrated surgeon and doctor. I was the only retinal surgeon in the entire province, providing care to one million people. I was extremely busy straight away. It was a private hospital and it was a concept that every year you build up your rights. In the first year I got a big fixed salary. The next year I received a percentage of profits. By the fourth year, I was an equal partner. I was a big money-making machine for my partners and the hospital as my super-specialised surgery was very lucrative.

Surgery is a technical craft and I was lucky to have found a speciality that suited me on every level.

I had been working on the most advanced cases in a remote hospital with machines that broke. Now I was working with the best staff imaginable and the most expensive, modern equipment.

Operating under these excellent conditions was a breeze!

There are so many elements that make a competent surgeon. It is a combination of many factors and I was lucky enough to have a few of them.

My fingers are fine and long and they are perfect for delicate microsurgery. I also have excellent hand-eye coordination. That's the anatomical part of it. I am also smart, I make fast decisions and I can perform under stress.

I didn't like orthopaedic surgery or bowel surgery. During orthopaedic training I was once told to hold a patient's leg. It was an amputation and they didn't tell me what was about to happen. The result was that on one of my first operations I was left holding a person's severed leg. That put me off orthopaedics for the rest of my career.

I wasn't strong enough for major surgery. But I was really good at plastic surgery which requires small micro movements. As a junior house doctor on call I sutured someone's severed finger back on and it lived. Sometimes the nurses would ask me to re-stitch the work that junior general surgeons had done. I apposed the wound edges in a natural position in order to make the scar less obvious and the outcome more aesthetic. I was called by the midwives to do deliveries at night when other doctors were sleeping. I was also good at operating on arteries and varicose veins.

I was also good at microsurgery. I am good at doing delicate work.

My first idea was to specialise in plastic surgery. However, I didn't like the thought of six years of general surgery, which I would have to endure first. So this was my thought process: I saw a big need for ophthalmologists and it suited all my talents. It also allowed me to do healing work in a way I enjoyed. I was not going to be left holding a limb again.

But on top of all of that I also had a life purpose that I was supposed to do this work!

My success was largely due to the fact that I was a technically strong surgeon with extensive experience. I was able to make fast assessments, make correct diagnoses and take effective action. But behind the scenes it was far more than that. I worked with Angels and with my inner sight. I worked with my patients' Angels. I worked with energy and spirit.

My work with my own spirit body was gathering strength. I was reading all I could on spirituality. I was working with Angels and higher beings on a nightly basis. And I was bringing it into my practice more and more as I got more confident in my connection to this world.

I prayed at the start of every workday.

I prayed every time an operation was going wrong.

I prayed before every surgery. I always said:

"Dear God, only bring me patients whom I can help. Don't make me do surgery if it won't benefit this patient."

I was on my path of spiritual growth. I was back with my friend Lieve and she drew me into the world of the gurus. I lapped it all up. I started studying the emotional and spiritual causes of physical ailments. One of the doctors whose work I studied had worked with a Flemish medium called Bernaerts. She would tell the medicos that most diseases did not have a physical origin but were rather caused by thought and emotions. I was fascinated when I saw her talk about this and I bought all her books. As a doctor the connection fascinated me. I loved the ideas and studied them all.

She also spoke of animals and the messages they bring.

Many years later during a period when I was studying for an exam, I kept on seeing and hearing kookaburras everywhere. Every morning as I drove off to work, I would notice a large brown-beige kookaburra staring at me somewhere in front of my house. On one occasion I stopped my car, turned down the window, looked at it and said "kookookookookakakakakaka" and the bird replied with a louder version of "kookookookookakakakaka" before flying off, insulted, as they are territorial birds. When I went for a run on the beach the bird was there. When I ran through the forest I bumped into a kookaburra sitting on a low branch hanging over the narrow path. I stopped in surprise and we had a staring competition for 15 minutes or so. I was fascinated by these beautiful birds and wondered what it meant that they were so constantly around me. After digging through cardboard boxes full of books I located the book What animals are trying to tell you and looked up Kookaburra. It said, "This is a time for study and exam preparation!" Darn right it was. At the time study was dominating my life and time. After I sat the test the Kookaburras disappeared. They became a rare sighting, just like for everyone else.

I had come across an amazing old book at a flea market in Cape Town, titled Macro Mind Power. It was full of visualisations and manifestations and I used it all the time.

I added to my skill set by studying Usui Reiki studies in Belgium. I loved it and did level one and two. I became Reiki Master in 2005, while doing a short stint back in South Africa.

The principles of Reiki are principles of healing that we did not get taught at medical school. I learned how to become an ego-less vessel for Divine Energy to work through me. The Universal Energy enters through my crown chakra (at the top of my head) from a place of Love and Gratitude, passes my heart and goes into my arms.

The healing energy then enters the patient through my hands. You get taught certain secret symbols that you draw with your hands in the air or on the patient's clothes for extra effect. The symbols look like Japanese writing. Mikao Usui, the father of this popular form of Reiki, was Japanese. When I had burnout I used Reiki healing energy on myself to boost my energy levels by putting my hands on my kidneys and adrenal glands. More and more I started to use the process of Reiki in my surgeries.

Reiki works on children and animals alike. I think we all do it unconsciously when we rub a sore spot or kiss a child's scratch better. I remember reviving little newborn kittens with my hands when I was only five and healing the front leg of my cat that was booked in for amputation. I did the same work recently on a dog with a broken leg. The vet had decided to amputate I put my hands on his leg for 20 minutes or so and the puppy still has four paws today.

Don't get me wrong: I don't think I am anything special. But as a doctor I started to tap into another way to heal people. Combined with my surgeon's scalpel it was amazing what happened.

I also started to call on many benevolent helpers or guides who are deceased surgeons. They assist me with their knowledge and experience.

All these light beings stand in a half circle behind my back as I perform surgery and speak through my mind and my hands. A friend who was an ophthalmologist in Cape Town died about 15 years ago in a car accident and I felt his presence for a few years after, helping me. But then he moved on.

I have found that most guides don't stay with you your whole life.. It depends on your mission, how are you serving the planet and what stage of your life and growth you are in.

There are also different Angels for different tasks. They even have described a hierarchy in the Angel world.

The third kind of helpers is ascended masters like Jesus and Buddha and Quan Yin and many more. These are enlightened beings that have chosen to continue to be of service to us earthlings, after their ascension.

Earlier in the book I mentioned how I saw a deceased loved one holding my patient's hand during surgery. She had smiled at me and said her name was Martha.

I often sense deceased loved ones around older people who are about to pass and I then get the message it will be the last time I will see this patient. I give them a good hug before they go and bless them with a happy afterlife (quietly in my head).

This turned out to be a correct intuition of mine on many occasions through my life: with patients but also with many family members.

If this happens I know I cannot change their fate. There is no healing so I focus on sending peace, love and acceptance of letting go, knowing it will be all good. They are off to a better place without the pain and discomfort of an ageing body.

CHAPTER 22

Climbing the ladder back in Bruges

On every level my life was skyrocketing. My career was on hyper drive. I was doing all the difficult cases. My colleagues gave me all the most complicated and highest paid cases. I had a lot of responsibility and appreciation and I was finally getting paid.

I worked with two other specialists and the three of us formed a practice.

One was an older Belgian ophthalmologist in his 50s who gave himself the title of department head. He was from a very well connected old Bruges family and had a lot of power. The second was younger, in his mid-40s, a young father, kinder and ambitious.

I had been working in Bruges for about a year when I walked past a store that I had never noticed before. The windows were enthralling with the cutest high fashion children's fashion such as baby Dior and little Armani. After I spent 15 minutes browsing and touching the delicate little baby outfits, I heard a voice saying … "It's time, I want to be born."

I knew it was my son calling me.

Well, I thought, if we are going to have a baby, I should consider marrying Mark. It was a thought that came out of nowhere.

That evening when I walked home Mark was waiting for me in the kitchen. As I walked in he did the strangest thing. He dropped on the floor, his eyes brimming with tears. Then he proposed to me. It was totally out of the blue. He didn't even have a ring. He said the urge to propose overcame him.

I said yes but I hesitated a little because I was a bit taken aback and the princess in me had wanted more glamour and a big diamond. I eventually bought my own!

We got married in the medieval Knights Hall in Bruges on 26 October 2002. A week later we had another wedding ceremony with a priest, barefoot in the beach sand of Brenton on Sea in South Africa. I felt my son Matthew's presence very strongly during the wedding ritual. It was mystical, with the sound of the cold waves crashing, and the fog spreading over the beach. Our 20 guests formed a circle around us on the beach. The reception was held afterwards in a white tent on the grass in front of the hotel. The tables were decorated beautifully in white with vases filled with shells. We said our vows on the very beach where I wrote my soulmate wish list the day I met Mark on the plane!

We tried for a baby immediately and to my surprise nothing happened for six months. I was 35 at the time. I went for a fertility test and it was all fine. Then Mark went and there was nothing really wrong with either of us. I got inseminated once but this was such an unpleasant experience involving a giant obstetrician on call with hands the size of shovels that I decided to let nature take its course. We went on a holiday and I decided not to stress. That's when it happened. Matthew's eager soul was sucked into our physical world, invited by our love energy. It felt like a big vortex of white light connected my crown to the divine, all-knowing source. I actually experienced an opening of crown, heart and second chakra inviting in the universal energy that would create this mini nuclear reaction in my womb. There and then energy transformed into matter like alchemy.

I had been working hard at my new medical practice for one-and-a-half years when I fell pregnant. But that single event was to change everything.

The problems really started in the second trimester of my pregnancy. Mark and I went on a self-drive tour through Mexico. Seeing the Incan and Aztec temples in the jungle was high on my wish list of travel destinations.

My obstetrician tried her best to persuade me to take a local break instead. As I had no idea how taxing the 'miracle pregnancy' would be for my 35-year-old body, I stubbornly stuck to our plans. I agreed to avoid the most dangerous drug-related violent areas. There had been incidences of tourists being held up and captured for ransom. Unfortunately I was having so much trouble breathing in the humid, hot air that I struggled to climb the two flights of steps to our beautiful suite that had a rooftop hot tub. Mark conquered the steep steps to the top of the pyramid shaped temples as I caught my breath while resting on the ancient big stones at ground level.

Even worse than my breathing problem was the fact that I could hardly walk. I kept telling my obstetrician but she told me that it was normal and it would come right. But it didn't come right. It got worse and worse. By the third trimester I was hardly able to walk at all.

I went from super-surgeon to working at half power overnight.

I was almost immobile and the hospital had to hire an assistant to walk up and down to get patients out of the waiting room for me. The pregnancy made me so exhausted I used to fall asleep at my desk.

What was even more bizarre was that my two older male colleagues were turning against me. They were men with stay-at-home wives. They had no compassion for the physical hardship I was enduring. Not even the female doctors were sympathetic. My own obstetrician told me I was lucky to get three weeks off as maternity leave, as she herself had only been given one week off with the birth of her third child. This was because I was a doctor and self-employed. I didn't get paid if I didn't work. The hospital and my two colleagues also missed out on a big share of my earnings while I was absent.

My body was falling apart. I felt more and more unmotivated at work as I felt unwelcome and unfairly judged as lazy. No one helped to push my heavy body uphill to the hospital entrance so I hobbled slowly behind my wheelchair.

I was falling out of love with my job and my life. All the things that used to boost my happiness levels: tennis, walks on the beach, and cycling had been taken away from me. Instead of enjoying exercise-induced endorphins I was experiencing constant pain in my pelvis and lower back. It stopped me from sleeping properly (I also started to have sleep apnoea).

My pregnancy got worse and worse.

I only found out years later during my second pregnancy that I had a condition called pelvic instability. They didn't diagnose it in my first pregnancy. It is a condition where your ligaments stretch so much that your pelvis actually splits. I could hardly stand up.

Despite all my problems I had decided I wanted a water birth. It had been a huge fight with Mark. While in Mexico we stayed in a tiny hotel that had a book on underwater deliveries. Strangely enough, the place where underwater deliveries were developed was in Belgium! I was on the other side of the world and there it was like an Angel Message. When I got back I tracked down the hospital where underwater births were done. The hospital was in Ostend, the next city to Bruges. I told Mark that I wanted to do it but he totally refused. He said he would not allow it. It was too far and I needed to go to the local hospital, where I worked. I was totally overruled by my husband. He wanted me to have a C-Section. No debate.

"You will not risk my son's life because you want to sit in a bath," Mark said. "I will not risk losing him or you," he said.

"I was born through a Caesarean and so was my brother and my mum is fine," he added to the pro C-Section argument.

"Your mother had a complete hysterectomy when you were born and fell into sudden early menopause because of that," I thought. "And she couldn't breastfeed you because she had too much pain and medication after such major surgery." But my lips remained zipped, as I didn't want Mark to get a complex about hurting his mum. She was a stoical woman with an excellent sense of humour who never ever complained

"Your pelvis is too narrow for the baby's head to pass through the birth canal," my obstetrician nodded as she looked at the X-rays I had taken ten minutes earlier. A good thing about Flemish private hospitals is that things get done quickly. Time is money.

In a public hospital members of staff get a fixed salary no matter how many patients they help. Because of this they are tempted to move as slowly as a turtle, which leads to cancelled tests and procedures…

I should have trusted my intuition.

Matthew was born on 17 December 2003 after a tormenting and complicated pregnancy during what was supposed to be a routine C-Section. It should have been a good day. Expecting our firstborn at the age of 35 was something to celebrate. I had also been promised that all my pain would go once I had delivered my baby.

CHAPTER 23
I crash and burn

It was supposed to be a routine C-Section. But as I lay tied to the operation table in the worst distress, pain, fear and anger, I knew that something was wrong.

"Anybody, please help me, anybody!" I screamed.

Mud brown negative clouds carrying the energies of disease, fear, anger and guilt floated towards me from all over the hospital.

I was in pain everywhere. Most of the pain came from my wrist.

My wrist was tied up with a leather strap against a hard wooden board angled at 45 degrees and the surgeon's first assistant pushed hard against it. I could feel the bones in my right hand dislocating. The medial wrist tendon was being stretched, and the repetitive nerve pain shot through my shoulder into my neck.

But they didn't listen to me. They didn't react to my numerous requests to move my wrist. They ignored me.

Instead they gave me more intravenous Propofol (the white liquid infamous for killing Michael Jackson) to shut me up.

Mark sat next to my head. We both wore light blue theatre hats. Mark wore green scrubs that contrasted strongly with his flushed red skin. He was scared and shocked at my distress.

His gentle light blue eyes stared at me and filled with tears as our baby boy was pulled out of my abdomen through the large gaping cut through skin, fat, muscle and finally my uterus.

Matthew, my little friend who had kept me company with his angelic energy and night time soccer kicks, opened his eyes and beamed his wise eyes at me. Then he blessed me with a good stream of urine.

I got to sniff my beautiful baby for only a few minutes. I felt as if I knew him. I felt that he recognised the sound of Mark's and my voice. I wanted to hold him but both my hands were tied. As they started scooping out the placenta and trying to limit the bleeding from my uterus my teary-eyed husband carried our child away to be weighed and measured. His health was quickly summarised in an Apgar score.

"I am left alone again," I think, unaware of the dark entities that were taking root as parasites inside my body.

Back in recovery and in the ward, I was still in agony. Was this normal? It was my first baby and I didn't know if the pain was normal or wrong. was All I knew was that I was in terrible pain. I just lay there, unable to move and not knowing what was wrong or what to do.

I asked to see a doctor as I had so much pain in my back. I was on a morphine pump. But I could feel that I had a huge bruise at the site of the epidural. The doctor on call said I needed it "looked at". Then I was diagnosed with a dislocated pelvis and wrist.

"Remind me, please, to never do this again," I whispered to Mark, exhausted.

Other women in my ward were happy and smiling and having fun. But I felt like I was living in a horror movie. Mark didn't know what has happening either and he didn't speak up. I felt more and more vulnerable. I was told I was a sissy. It was the worst thing that had ever happened to me in all my life. I am one tough cookie but this was just the worst thing I had experienced and I didn't understand why it was happening to me.

Basically the doctors had made a massive mess out of my operation and no one ever told me. They had dislocated my wrist and pelvis and the epidural had caused a massive bleeding in my spinal cord as well as a leak of cerebrospinal fluid.

Then my C-section wound got infected!

I was sent home and Mark had to stop work to take care of the baby. I lay in bed for my entire three weeks maternity leave and could not move or do a thing. Mark kept Matthew away from me, thinking he was doing me a favour and letting me rest and heal. But I wanted to be close to my baby and I got increasingly frantic.

Just before the end of my three weeks leave I received a phone call from the head of the department, my oldest colleague: The Boss. He told me I had to come in to perform an intravitreal injection of antibiotics on a patient. The patient was his own uncle and he feared that he had an endophthalmitis. This is an infection that can cause blindness and it's caused by the eye filling with pus after an operation.

I didn't want to go and made that clear.

"I am still on pregnancy leave," I said. "Can't another colleague do it?" His voice was threatening and so I ended up dragging myself into the hospital theatre and did as I was told.

That single act of objection set in motion a chain of events I could never have predicted.

"This is not an endopthalmitis," I told the boss after I examined the patient at the slit lamp. It was a complicated surgery and I was in agony.

I went back to work when my three weeks were up in a wheelchair. I couldn't move my right hand. My colleagues told me I was making it up. I had to show them the ultrasound that showed the tendinitis in my right wrist and other medical certificates.

I always thought I had a super body until I got pregnant. I was athletic. I knew I could do anything! I had won tennis competitions and I could play any sport. But now I was falling apart physically and I was told it was all psychosomatic.

I had to produce the anatomical evidence of all my injuries. I had to prove through scans that I had a leak in my spinal cord from the lumbar puncture. I wore a brace to support my right hand for a month. I had physiotherapy that didn't help and finally a steroid injection into the tendon sheath. That helped. But what about the pelvic instability and the hip dislocation?

I went back to work on week three in a wheelchair. They had taken away my assistant so nobody could push me up the ramp to the entrance.It was hard. Nobody helped me. They stared at me like I was a hypochondriac, laughing behind my back. Not one human being was willing to help. I was so hurt and disappointed in mankind.

I had lost my connection to my Angels.

During the C-section when I cried for help and called for anybody, lot of dark energies jumped into me. But I only was to find this out later. Hospitals have plenty of negative entities and imprints that have been left behind by disease. That is why you should always protect yourself with a ball of white light when you visit someone in hospital. You don't want to take any of those dark energies home.

During my pregnancy I communicated and felt very close to my baby Matthew inside of me. It was like having a constant friend and companion. He would kick me awake when I had problems breathing at night. He was very restless during the last full moon before his birth almost as if the forces of nature were pulling him out of me. Even though my baby was ready to come out, it didn't happen as his head was much too big to pass through the birth canal.

All the time during the birth I didn't speak to my Angels. I was fearful and scared and I couldn't connect to them at all. I didn't pray. I was scared and in a dark place. I forgot all my links and connections. Either I felt it coming or I created it with my feelings. I am not sure but in hindsight I know I didn't trust my intuition and I got lost. I didn't listen to all the clues.

One of the mediums I knew had even driven all the way from Brussels to Bruges twice to give me this haunting message: "You should NOT deliver your baby in the hospital where you work. Things will go terribly wrong. You will suffer the consequence and pain for a very long time after."

I have saved so many others and myself over the years by listening to my Angels, guides and intuition. I DIDN'T want to go to that hospital but Mark was determined. I was fragile and in a wheelchair and I couldn't fight back.

CHAPTER 24

A downhill spiral

Once I had Matthew and was officially back at work, what was a tenuous work situation during my last trimester was now an open war zone.

I was working five days a week plus I was on call every three nights. And they were very long workdays.

I wasn't coping at all so I again asked to have a half-day off every week. They refused.

"That is not why we hired you," the older doctor told me.

"We can't afford that," said others. They were running a busy practice and working around the clock. They didn't want a colleague not pulling her weight - but I was unable to work at my former pace.

We fought and fought and eventually I won the half-day off, but the cost was high. I was no longer one of them. I was the enemy. But I felt as if I had been the enemy for some time, ever since I fell pregnant.

They gave me the half-day off but they said I was not a fully participating member of the practice any more. They cut off my benefits and trimmed my salary - "recalculating the lesser percentage I should get now that I worked less".

I had an attorney to represent me, but this didn't progress. Increasingly they were putting me in a tighter and tighter corner. I was sure they had meetings about me behind closed doors.

At the same time that I was fighting to save my career, I was struggling with two major physical conditions that floored me. The first was that the pain in my pelvis had not cleared up after the delivery as everyone had promised. In fact it was just as bad. But the second was a terrible exhaustion that threatened to keep me in bed every weekend.

A physiotherapist was trying to help with pelvic disability. It had not yet been diagnosed as that so all I knew was that walking was difficult and lifting was painful. The pain in my lower back was so severe it woke me up several times a night. What we didn't know was that my entire pelvis was out and my muscles were in spasm, trying to pull it back. The physiotherapist treated the symptoms and sent me to an osteopath.

But the pain didn't clear and only got worse. For an entire year I could not walk unassisted. I had never taken time off work.

Every step I took was sore and difficult. It was a ten-metre walk to go and call a patient from the waiting area to my office. That walk took me forever.

I was told it was all in my head. I produced X-rays showing the pelvic misalignment.

As a result of the damage done to my right wrist during my C-Section, I had to wear a splint, which meant I couldn't operate for a month. Not being able to operate meant I made less money for my colleagues and the entire practice. There was less profit for all of us as all the income was pooled and divided.

And so, after an ultrasound confirming inflammatory fluid in my wrist tendon I had a steroid injection in it. This cleared up the pain over the next few days so I could leave the splint and go back to operating. My right hand, however, has always remained weaker and has less muscle mass. I have adapted to doing most heavy lifting with my left hand.

More concerning than the pain in my pelvis and wrist was the terrible and debilitating exhaustion that I felt.

It wasn't just the normal exhaustion a new mother has. I was so tired some days I could hardly get out of bed. I could not even lift my head up.

I was so run down that my general practitioner eventually booked me off for a week's bed rest. This was something I had never done before in my life. Being the patient instead of the doctor made me feel very uncomfortable.

I went from doctor to doctor to try and get help.

I was so low and exhausted that I went to see a specialist at the Institute for Tropical disease, thinking that I may have contracted something during all my years in Africa. He did all the tests and then he said:

"I think you have burnout just like my wife."

I saw an anti-aging doctor in Antwerp and he ran many blood tests. He tested me for adrenal fatigue. At least he did the right tests: measured 24-hour cortisol in my urine and examined the flora in my stool. He told me the right things:

"Your entire system is out of whack. Your adrenal glands are exhausted."

"What do I do now?" I asked, feeling lost.

He gave me melatonin and adrenal support supplements to take.

I saw a homeopathic doctor.

"Everything starts in the intestines," he told me. It didn't make much sense to me at that stage. I understand what he meant now. He picked up on all my food allergies and gave me homeopathic treatment against those allergens. That was not the first time that came up in my disease history. Food allergies to dairy, wheat and other food components commonly cause inflammation of the gut and the rest of the body. It is a recognised part of adrenal fatigue. Adrenal fatigue is the physical version of emotional burnout, in my opinion.

I saw a rheumatologist in Bruges who confirmed the pelvic misalignment but her orthopaedic solution caused a lot of hip pain. I couldn't tolerate that pain.

I was advised by some of the doctors to claim on my income protection insurance and the insurance company sent me to see a general practitioner in order to get a letter confirming my condition. The fact that his office was on the first floor was not a coincidence and there was no lift! I had to drag myself up his stairs to his office. I am convinced that was done on purpose as a test to sort out the quacks from the seriously impaired.

He was supposed to assess me for burnout.

At one point during the consultation he pushed down on my pubic bone making me scream in pain.

"I think, I know what is wrong with you," he whispered.
He then wrote a report advising my insurance company that I didn't suffer from chronic fatigue and could continue working.

I was getting increasingly despondent with my own profession – the doctors and specialists who were supposed to bring me back to health. I could see that they didn't know anything. I was clearly a woman in severe pain but because they didn't have a label for it, they told me it was psychosomatic.

CHAPTER 25
Modern medicine misdiagnosed me

The only healers who really helped me at that time were ones outside traditional medicine.

I found refuge with a psychologist, spiritual healers, physiotherapists, osteopaths, and shiatsu and reiki therapists.

I was already long on the path of studying the connection between the body and the mind and I was searching for ways to heal myself. My search took me into the world of Belgian alternative healers.

I visited a medium who gave me Bach flower remedies and drops. It helped me with the emotional trauma. We did mediations together. That is when I first found the Void and Christ Consciousness. Then I met a naturopath. The kind man from the organic vegetable store in St Michiels referred me to her.

Veronique was to become my mentor and friend and my closest ally over the next few years.

Veronique had an ethereal energy, as if she was from another planet, another dimension.

She was very tall and very tiny boned, fragile and often ill. She had shoulder-length brown curly hair and kept her hands busy. She always looked immaculate in beautiful new silky clothes from a Belgian designer.

Both Veronique and her husband, who wore his long glossy black hair in a ponytail like a North American Indian, were vegetarians and cooked only organic food. Vero gave long hugs when we said goodbye after a treatment. She would hold my face against her soft mohair sweater and slowly rub her hand over my back as to open my heart chakra for receiving.

The first three appointments I made with her over the phone were cancelled because she had a migraine. I had hoped that she could have helped save my career in Bruges.

On my first visit to her home, I had to wait for ages before she opened the door. She was running overtime with her previous client. When I first saw Veronique, I thought she was a weirdo: she spoke softly and exuded love and was always kind.

That day I stepped from an aggressive male world at work into Venus' treatment room.

During our first hour together she used NLP on me (neurolinguistic programming). During the session I walked back on my life's timeline to find happy Veerle and brought her back with me into the present. I also visited unhappy baby Veerle walking alone through dark streets and I held her hand so that she would never be scared in the dark again. I found this to be a very powerful way of healing past negative events. I got to rewrite my past, creating a happier present and a better future.

Veronique used her third eye and her spirit guides to look at the conflict with my colleagues and tried to heal it. One day after a session, she opened her door and we both saw a red robin on the ground, with his heart ripped out of his chest.

She nodded. "These people are very powerful,", Veronique said.

I found in Veronique a teacher who was walking the same spiritual path as me. She understood when I told her about Angels and other spiritual beings. She knew Angels too. So finally I had found someone I could talk to about my world.

Once I knew that modern medicine was not going to help me I realised that I had to help myself.

I was on a steep learning curve to develop my own intuition. I know that we all co-create our life. Our thoughts, emotions, the things we say with conviction as well as our beliefs, create our future.

I had to look deeply into my own life.

Was this happening to me because I never really wanted to come and work and live in Belgium again? I had accepted the job under pressure of Mark and some colleagues and friends. It had never been my heart's desire to leave my favourite rainbow country: South Africa.

Did my own negative thoughts cause these traumatic events, on a physical level?

Was getting sick and run down actually my way out of this place?

Was it serving me in some way?

Veronique did a year's course of lessons for a group of 20 health practitioners on how to tap into your psychic ability. I didn't do it all but I did many classes with them. I learned to open my third eye and to investigate my own past lives.

As my eyes opened to another world of energy and influence, I started to see that I was under a powerful psychic attack from my colleagues. They had thrown energy daggers in my back and neck. This damaged me energetically and I have no doubt that this contributed to my illness.

I worked hard with Veronique to develop ways to protect and heal myself.

I protected myself at work by using white light. I filled my aura with it and then I put a green glass cover over myself. If that didn't help I would visualise a cylinder of mirrors surrounding me, reflecting any negativity back to its origin. Lieve had taught me that protective technique. "Don't forget to close it at the top and bottom," she had said. I did this every morning.

Every day before I had to face my colleagues I filled myself with divine light and put on my green cover and my mirrors!

One morning I had a scheduled meeting with one of my partners in his office. I was very scared to actually have to confront him face to face. I arrived and waited half an hour for him before I went to look for him. I asked one of the staff where he was. She told me that he had become ill out of the blue and had been on the toilet for half an hour.

I started laughing hysterically. I knew it was the mirrors. They had reflected his attack right back at him. This was my first shield I had used and he was feeling the consequences. The orthoptist asked why I was laughing and I told her about the mirrors. I described to her what I had done to protect myself from him and I grinned: "It seems he is getting the bad vibes he was sending me right back at him."

She must have told him what I said because rumours started circulating about me being a witch. I think he thought I had put a curse on him while I had only been reflecting his negative thoughts in order to protect myself. In fact this small act of self-defence turned into a far bigger incident over time. This little rumour ruined my career in Belgium and still affects me to this day. A simple visualisation technique such as a protective bubble was strange and "demonic" to them. Decades later I heard that this inflated story had travelled from Belgium to South Africa and then it again reared its head in Australia. I felt as if these people have followed me around the globe energetically (and physically) for the last ten years! I realise now that my alternative ways were confronting to them, and they didn't understand me and that was threatening to them. At heart they were all good people, but we clashed on a professional level.

My intuition was starting to change the way I lived my life. I listened closely to it now. And one morning it called me loudly.

I was not hiding that I was interested in alternative healing. I was openly into readings and meditations and chanting Tibetan chants and drums. I was open-minded and spiritual. This was what was making me heal and feel human again and I was going for it!

It was a normal weekday and I had the morning off because I had a medical appointment with my physiotherapist who was treating me for my back.

Both her and my psychologist in Ostend were trying to convince me to quit my job because the animosity from my colleagues and the stress of an uncertain future were killing me (his exact words).

I felt better after my physiotherapy session and so I decided to go to work early. I was only expected in the afternoon. I walked into the clinic that day feeling upbeat. I noticed that the waiting room was not overflowing as usual. The waiting room was guaranteed to be packed at any hour of the day. There were about 20 uncomfortable plastic patient chairs. On the days the three of us were consulting at the same time they were all full. Some were patients but there were always 'the extras'. They were usually the accompanying drivers left standing next to their father or granny with cataracts, macular degeneration or diabetic retinopathy.

But today the room stood empty. This was very strange. I walked to the front desk office to ask one of the secretaries or medical staff what was happening.

"Where is everybody?"

"They are having a meeting with the hospital board," she said, looking at her feet.

"What!" I exclaimed. "I told them I couldn't be present today because of my medical appointments and asked for another date for the board meeting!"

"I don't think that message was passed on. They are going ahead without you."

As she spoke I knew something was wrong. My instincts were on high alert.

I felt a very physical response kick in. My body was shaking. Something was going on and I knew it.

"Fight, Veerle. Fight back!" it said.

I raced up the narrow staircase to the main entrance area towards the boardroom. I crashed down the door - at least that is what it felt like to me.

The boardroom was filled with the hospital's Medical Board, a group consisting of the department heads of each field of medicine. Amongst other decisions, these people had the right to vote doctors in or out of the hospital. Unlike in most Anglo-Saxon countries (United Kingdom, South Africa and mostly the United States) the power still lies in doctors' hands in Belgian hospitals more than in the hands of administrative staff and management. This means that doctors make the choices rather than those who have no clue about medicine. Non-medical managers generally make profitable choices rather than having the patients' and staff's wellbeing at heart.

Sitting in front of me was a group of about ten doctor representatives. Standing in front of them were my partners and it was clear that they were making a case against me! I had stumbled upon an attempted coup against me, and I hadn't been invited.

My intuition had led me straight into this. I stood my ground in front of everyone.

"You knew I wasn't able to attend this meeting and you went ahead anyway? Without me present? Accusing me!"

"Tell me what have they accused me of?" I looked around the room for some support. The psychiatrist, who was a gentle soul, explained:

"They are saying that you didn't come to the hospital twice when you were expected to attend to a casualty." Embarrassed, he lowered his gaze.

"That is totally ridiculous."

"Give me the dates, come on," I challenged my colleagues.

"You didn't want to come when I asked for your help with my uncle who got an infection after I operated his cataract," the old boss said.

"You called me three weeks after my son Matthew was born, on a Saturday. I was NOT on call but you still expected me to come and save you. And yes, I didn't want to ... because as head of the department and as a cataract surgeon I feel that you should be able to deal with your surgical complications yourself. You should be the one administering the antibiotic treatment when you have caused an infection in your patient! By the way, I did go into hospital as requested that day. I administered the antibiotics into the eye of his uncle, even though I didn't agree with his diagnosis or treatment. I wasn't even on call. The question here should be why a department head can't do such a small procedure himself!

I ended on a high note.

The room was silent. I think they were scared of seeing the Veerle Dragon producing more heat and fire as the minutes went by.

"What is the next accusation?" I asked, looking around towards my shaky audience. My younger colleague, a nice man and an excellent surgeon and ophthalmologist, stepped forward:

"There was that time when I called you on a Wednesday afternoon to have a look at a patient with a retinal detachment and you didn't come."

"You called me on my day off, while I was visiting my friend in the Netherlands. So officially I was NOT on call and NOT even in the country! I can't be available for you and your patient's 365 days a year! I also deserve some time off!"

"But the patient was anxious," he replied.

"That is understandable," I replied. "I went to see her the next morning but she wasn't there.

"I sent her to the University of Leuven and they operated on her the next day."

"Voila, I rest my case. That is exactly what I asked you to do. I told you to admit her and that I would examine and operate on her the next day."

"So what is this REALLY about?" I searched the circle for an honest face.

The rest of the board members were impressed by my defence and moved on and returned to their wards.

I was relieved that I had won this battle but my fire had ignited something way bigger in my boss. He was gathering twigs to use for the ultimate burning of the witch - me!

I walked out that day feeling somewhat vindicated that I had said my piece after so many months of accusations. It was out in the open and there was something of a relief in that. It had been an opportunity to confront, head-on, what felt at the time like a really nasty campaign against me.

The stress of facing work every day was so huge it was making me ill. I was edgy, worried, and could not sleep.

What would I do if I lost my job? I had a child and a husband with no job.

I was already seeing a psychologist. He was eventually very firm with me.

"Veerle, if you cannot even have a normal conversation with your employers you need to leave."

But this was not an easy choice. I had worked for four years building a practice. I had invested my time and my money in this translocation. I was officially a partner. It would be crazy to walk away from all of that. It had been a hard slog but I was finally there.

I was a full partner by then. I had worked my way up in the practice for four full years, working to a gruelling schedule.

I didn't want to resign. Giving in is not in my nature. I am a fighter. But my psychologist eventually gave me an ultimatum.

"If you don't leave that workplace, you are going to get really sick and you won't be able to continue working," he warned. "Your future actually depends on you walking away from this level of stress."

Mark was pushing me too.

"Just leave and we will make a plan," he told me.

I knew I had to do it but quitting was against my nature. I didn't want to give up; I didn't want to let go. I wanted to fight them and show them up. But everyone was telling me to back down. They told me it was not worth it and that I would get sicker and sicker from the stress.

On the day I planned to resign there was a song on the radio by the British girlband SugaBabes: "Stronger! You are not alone! You are getting stronger!" The lyrics touched my heart and tears started flowing down my cheeks. I knew this was a sign. I knew I should keep fighting for my career, my reputation and my job. I wanted to keep going.

But everyone who loved me was telling me to back off. So I decided to trust them and finally accept that it was over.

I was due to meet my boss that day and I was on time for our meeting. He was due to present me with a new financial contract. As I walked into his office, he was sitting at his desk. He didn't even really look up before he started talking to me about a proposal he had for me. Another work contract.

I sat down in front of him and he started to discuss the new proposal.

I cut him short.

"I am not interested in any proposal from you and here is my resignation." He looked up, surprised.

"Well, that's good news!" he said.

He could not even bother to hide his relief. Neither could I.

In resigning I had lost all the money I was still due for four years of work. It was such a blow, but I was so emotionally low that I had lost my fight by then.

Leaving this job was a huge setback to me at a time when I was already so low.

I had loved my job and I had based my future on it.

I had built up a career and I was a huge success. I had put everything into it. I was friends with the staff and others in Bruges. I had a beautiful home, a social life, a comfortable income, and a successful career. I felt it was my dream job. I had my own office and exciting medical cases and surgeries.

It all went haywire because I wanted to work one half-day less a week because I had a tiny baby!

I have huge willpower and emotional strength. I can stand in any battle until I fall. I wanted to fight to the death but the psychologist told me to get out. Mark told me to get out.

I felt as if my Angels had deserted me during this entire time. I was stuck in the trenches of a battle and I hadn't turned to them to get out. Instead, I had turned to lawyers and doctors. But none of them had helped me at all. When you wallow in negative thoughts and emotions like hate, anger, revenge your vibration is too far removed from the ethereal energy of Angels and light beings. They are there but you can't hear or see them from those lower planes.

So eventually I followed everyone's advice but my own and I got out.

But when I left for good I wasn't sad. I was angry. Anger is an emotion that hides sadness. Deep down I was sad that I hadn't been able to make it work. I had left behind our beautiful home, my motherland, friends and my successful vitreo retinal career with a great salary.

CHAPTER 26

A place to heal

During the last few months of my tenure my thoughts had turned back to South Africa. I knew both Mark and I could go back to our old jobs.

I called my professor back at Pretoria Academic.

"Come back, we miss you," he said.

I didn't need to be asked twice. We left Belgium in December 2004, just after Matthew's first birthday. I was free and excited to move back to South Africa – Mark's home and the country we both loved.

We moved into a secure complex in Pretoria as I got ready to go back to work. But there was a hold-up in my paperwork and it turned out that I had to wait six months to get back to work.

These were the six months that I needed. Matthew was a year and a half.

I could finally spend time with him.

I danced with Matthew and we played all day. We went everywhere together and had lots of fun. He was happy and easy. It was a very healing time for me. I hadn't had this time with my son. It was the best thing I have ever done – finally I was getting some emotional healing.

My body started to heal. I found a great osteopath and chiropractor. He diagnosed me with pelvic instability. Finally somebody knew what was wrong and why I was in so much pain. He treated me every week and I slowly started to get better.

My disillusionment with the medical world grew deeper. I started to question whether doctors are healers at all. I was spending my days consulting and fixing people's vision but increasingly I was finding that healing was not what doctors offered, including me.

I was delving deeper into spiritual healing for myself. But I was also finding that more and more I was using these esoteric techniques during surgery.

We all have healing powers and we all have benevolent helpers from other dimensions who are eager to come and help. All you have to do is to just ask!

Once I started asking it became the way I did surgery and the way I healed patients. My surgery felt as if it was guided by a force greater than me, a universal energy that I gave myself over to.

I was diving deep into new worlds and my next step was to have "psychic surgery" on my own wounds.

I had just met an older, 60-something, German lady, Gerlinde, who was also a spiritual healer.

"It is not a coincidence that you have met me on your first week in the country and your first visit to the school," Gerlinde told me with her noticeable German accent.

"What do you mean?" I asked.

"We were meant to meet here today," she answered. "My spirit guides sent me here and told me you would be waiting." We started working together on my healing.

She did psychic surgery on me. She scraped out the negative energy I had attracted during the C-section. Each session took more than an hour. I lay on a massage table while Gerlinde held her hands over my body, whispering the Reiki words and writing the Reiki symbols in my aura.

The process was remarkable. I could see dark, muddy and stringy energy being pulled out of my body. They were sticky patches, thick like black tar and attached to my internal organs. It was like a black spider web. It was everywhere. It was hard to get rid of.

Gerlinde had to repeat the process about three times to clear it. Other times we meditated and she finished my Reiki training. I became a Reiki Master myself that year. The flow of Universal energy that enters my crown, flows through my heart and exits my hands when I touch anything that needs healing. I felt a strong pull to clear myself on all levels of negative energies

I had picked up during the previous year.

After my work with her I felt clearer and cleaner. I felt that a lot of the negativity had gone. Stuff that wasn't me was gone. I was starting to feel more like myself.

Gerlinde introduced me to some of my long-term spirit guides and Ascended Masters. She also passed on messages to me from masters like from Master Kuthumi.

"He likes the red nail colour on your toes as the colour red helps you to ground and receive earth energy. This way you pull in your soul from all corners and become more present in your body. You are then in a position of clarity where you can make better choices."

Or

"He likes your Asian style decor at home."

"What the…!" I thought. Gerlinde had never been to my home so how did she know that my black leather couch, red lacquer square cupboard and bright red carpet were inspired by Asia?

It was the first time I even noticed that myself. Aha! I realised that I had bought what my spirit guide liked! So much for free will.

After six months of waiting to get my work visa Matthew went to kindergarten and I went back to work. I couldn't work full-time as I was still very weak.

My own healing was following an intuitive road and I was finally in the driver's seat. I wasn't waiting for doctors to tell me what to do. Finally I felt as if I knew how to heal. I was following a path I could feel deeply was the right one for me.

I found a South African female naturopathic doctor who treated me for chronic fatigue, burnout and adrenal exhaustion. She had a treatment room full of patients of all ages, sitting on couches and receiving energy boosting cocktails via a drip into their veins. Others received detoxifying infusions that leeched heavy metals from their bodies.

There was a huge difference in her attitude to the doctors I had called on in Belgium. It was the first time a doctor took me seriously. She looked at my fresh blood sample under a microscope. The picture of my live moving blood cells was projected onto a TV screen for me to see. She showed me the rouleaux, which are red blood cells that stick together so that they can't carry oxygen through the body. She also showed me unhealthy fat globules in my blood sample that were a sign of a badly functioning pancreas and liver (the main detoxification organ). This is not the same as cholesterol. I have never had bad readings on my traditional blood tests, except for a raised level of inflammation (ESR means erythrocyte sedimentation rate) in which inflammation in my blood was causing my red blood cells to stick together and sink to the bottom of the test tube faster than was acceptable for my age. Inflammation and sticky blood and less oxygen to your organs is part of aging. But I was only 35 and had a one-year-old baby boy to care to look after for the next 20 years!

This doctor and her staff could see I was a woman in distress, and they responded to me in a respectful and caring manner.

So I moved forward at a furious pace finding these different ways to heal.

I had ozone therapy weekly. I was in the end-stage adrenal fatigue and this was one thing that really helped me. This was giving my organs a boost of oxygen, which was lacking because of my sticky red blood cells. But there was a big problem. The only oxygen sessions available were on Tuesdays. Tuesday was the main day I had been hired to operate on retinas.

It was Mark who pushed me to put myself first.

"Veerle you have to do this. You are more important than your work. You have a family and I also need you to be healthy and okay," he told me. He was right.
So I told them, at my brand new job, that I could not work on Tuesdays.

It was not a good way to start. It was a huge inconvenience for them – which I knew and which was why it was such a hard choice for me. They had to find someone to take my place. So what happened is that the junior doctors did the operations. They only called me if there was a terrible complication. The juniors didn't like me. They didn't want a 35-year-old woman to come in and save the day. So a very conflictual relationship developed between me and the rest of the male staff. Again!

In fact, the job was very different now. There was a pack of new younger male registrars and it was harder. They wanted to learn and get as many operations under their belt as they could. For most of the time I had to stand and watch while they did the surgery. They didn't want me to operate! I had no authority any more.

Again, I was the only woman doctor on the staff. I was competing with men and I was a new mother battling burnout. There was an Indian lady but she fell pregnant and had to stop working. It was only the nurses and admin staff that were female.

I also got a feeling that the rumours from Belgium had found their way to South Africa.

One young man told me he had met my Belgian colleagues and he told me that they had told him that I was a witch. He said he had heard that I had done all these "terrible things" and that I had "put a curse on a colleague". The small protective visualisation was coming back to haunt me!

Email to Véronique

Tonight I had a dream that Mark was married to someone else and that made me very sad, almost panicky. I felt a strong longing in my heart to be married to him. I missed him too the weekend Matthew and I visited the seaside with my friend Alet. We are a good trio: Mark, Matthew and I. I hope that the energy between Mark and me can be healed. I wish he would allow you to do some energy work on him too.

I haven't been able to capture the same happiness I felt the first time I lived in South Africa. Even though the time I spend with Matthew is wonderful, the responsibility that comes with parenthood contradicts my freedom-loving spirit. There is also a strong drive to express my true self to the world.

I hope to find a balance once I go back to work. The ideal job hasn't materialised yet. The dream of living in Australia keeps on haunting me though.

But it also shows what damage a small rumour can do in this unwelcoming world of medicine. The truth was that I was a powerful and creative being. I talked to Angels and I would use their help in my work. I prayed morning and night.

CHAPTER 27
Back in Africa

The local South African doctors were strangely hostile to me. But there were a lot of foreign doctors working in the hospital. They accepted me. They could see my skill set and appreciated me, but the South African doctors put their egos first. It was crazy. It felt like every surgery was a fight about who could do this and that.

I realised that it had always been an Old Boys Club. But during my first four years in training here, I had been so powerful. I had been a fighter and I had taken them on. That is how I got so far in my vitreo-retinal career. But this time I wasn't so strong. I didn't have the energy left to fight them.

I did my work but it didn't give me as much pleasure. They gave me the jobs others didn't want.

I stayed in my position for a year and a half but most of the time I was not happy there. So I kept an eye out for other job offers.

When I figured out that my career was going nowhere in South Africa I also had to look deeply at myself. Something in me was sabotaging my own career.

I started to look for other jobs more seriously. It had been my lifelong dream to go to Australia. As a child I had watched an Australian TV series called The Flying Doctors and that had been a huge inspiration for me during medical school. I had always had a romantic idea of myself being a flying doctor helping people out in rural areas. I knew that my options in South Africa were limited so I turned my attention to that side of the world.

Véronique

I met a German Reiki master at the Philosophy school. We meet weekly for spiritual teachings. I find the vibrational energy of my group in the Philosophy school quite low. I go to the gym every day and that makes me very tired. Then I give myself Reiki, putting my hands on my kidneys and adrenal glands gives me an enormous boost of energy. Than I fall asleep and awake refreshed an hour later.

The biggest stress comes from a lack of money at the moment. That is why I want to go back to work but at this stage that is not feasible yet. Australia keeps on spooking through my head.
I dreamt that Mark was spinning energy worms to me and I had to use anger and willpower to disconnect him from me.
The days after I felt a lot better but Mark became tired in turn. During sex he made new attachments. I want to limit this energy drain but then his mood drops even lower. Can you disconnect us energetically, please?
I also dreamt that my old evil Belgian colleague is trying to sabotage everything for me in South Africa again.
Please, bring the Angel bumper sticker.
I would love to read a book about Angels.
I miss our spiritual evenings together.
Can't wait for your arrival.
Veerle

I had asked Veronique to visit us in South Africa from Bruges. She wasn't just my teacher and psychic healer but she was also my close friend. She stayed with us for two lovely weeks and it was like balm to my soul. She did healing on me every day working with Angels. There was one very powerful cleaning where we invoked four Archangels. I was sitting in the middle of my red carpet just feeling the power and the love of them around me. She asked them to clear any blockages holding me back from finding a new job and realising my dream of living in Australia.

That very night (only a few hours after the clearing) I received three emails with job offers from Australasia.

Thank you so much, Veronique!

Mark had a dream that stuff streamed out of an opening in the back of his neck. What does this mean? He is acting very distant and mentioned that our relationship has many flaws. He doesn't like the fact that I value other people's opinion (mainly yours) more than his. He has an appointment tomorrow to see the psychologist. She is a wise woman. I feel strong enough to make a decision for myself now. You are the only one who still has an influence on my decisions and this should also lessen.

The psychologist made me do that test today, like you see in some movies, where they show you prints of ink blotches and you tell them what you see.

She discussed one of the cards already. It showed that I have wings. She said that I had to make sure that I wish to fly away to Australia for a good reason and not to get away from Mark.

I'll keep you posted about the developments. I am flying to Tasmania to check out a job offer in Hobart, Tasmania, tomorrow. Love and Sunshine to you, Veerle

I flew to Tasmania this week for a job interview.

I hated it. It was too cold and wet and I didn't want to live there. I may as well be in Belgium. There was no good shopping there either.

I felt the same with a job offer in New Zealand.

As I flew home from Tasmania I got chatting to an Australian stranger in the airport. I told him about my trip and that I felt it was too wet and too cold in Tasmania.

He agreed. I asked, "Where is the best place to stay in the whole of Australia?"

"Queensland," he said. I filed that thought as good advice.

I told the recruitment company that I wanted to be on a beach where the sun shines. Every night I sat and dreamed and planned and did visualisations for this place. I put my hands on my kidneys giving myself Reiki energy every day and I built myself up. I visualised the future I wanted to create for myself.

The next appealing offer was in a small town called Hervey Bay, on the Queensland Coast of Australia. The words from the man I had met at the airport echoed in my mind.

They wanted to fly me out to see the town and we decided to make a holiday of it.

It was Christmas 2005 and Matthew was two when we got on the plane to Australia to visit Hervey Bay. We flew into Brisbane and took the northern highway up to Hervey Bay the next day. The town was a three-and-a-half hour drive and my first impression was that it was a bit of a backwater.

Ten years on I did not change that opinion!

The town itself is a collection of four fishing villages and the main industry is tourism. It is famous for its whale watching. Mark hated it on sight. It had all the things he didn't like being a sandy redhead: glaring sunshine.

It was Mark's worst kind of place – a town where most of the conversation was about whether to shop at Bunnings or Big W.

But the hospital was great. I met the manager and a few of the doctors working there. It was a big operation that not just serviced the town but also a larger surrounding area containing about 100 000 people.

The hospital manager took us for dinner in a restaurant right on the beach. As the service was really slow, my two-year-old son and I walked down to the shore. There was a full moon reflecting magically from the flat Coral Sea. While Matthew threw little pieces of coral in the moonlit ocean for the splash effect, I had a conversation with God.

"What should I do?" I asked.

Is there anything wrong with this place? I heard.

I shook my head.

"No."

Well take it then, He said.

The dinner went well.

I was lukewarm. If I was honest I told myself that the town was not great but it was okay. Nice beach, nice atmosphere and warm sunny weather but that was about it.

The hospital manager had lined up three architect firms that wanted to hire Mark in Hervey Bay. Neither of us loved the place, but nor did we hate it. It was just average on all levels.

I accepted the job.

We flew back to South Africa and started packing up. But the process was not as easy as we thought. The paperwork for Australia took almost a year to come through. So we only got back to Australia a year later, at the end of December 2006.

Mark and I resigned from our jobs and had packed up our lives in South Africa by June. We decided to enjoy some time in Belgium and we spent six months at my parent's house waiting for the work visa to come through. We had a bit of a honeymoon period. That's when I fell pregnant with Thomas in Amsterdam.

I knew the exact feeling the moment I conceived Thomas.

As we had sex I knew it was happening NOW. I felt all my chakras connecting between Mark and me in a loop between both of us. I felt an opening up inside my belly and our hearts connecting. In my head it looks like a big white light downloading. My orgasm felt like a nuclear reaction or explosion more than just physical. I felt it both times – with both Matthew and Thomas. It is the soul of the baby that comes into the mother's womb at that magical moment of co- creation. We were not using any contraception and I was 38 at the time.

It was a good time for me to fall pregnant. I had become a lot healthier. My body had recuperated during the years in South Africa with all the healing, dairy- and wheat-free eating, ozone therapy, shiatsu massage and working deeply on myself. I was connected daily to my Angels and guides.

I had worked with some really good healers so I was stronger and healthier. I had been on a prolonged holiday. I was in high spirits and about to go to the life of my dreams in Australia.

And so I was in the early stages of my second pregnancy when we arrived in December.

The hospital helped us find a small three-bedroom house in a complex. It was very similar to a security complex you would find in South Africa. But this one was really badly done. The walls were so thin that we could hear everything the neighbours were saying.

They fought at night, watched loud TV at 3am and had a yapping little dog. I couldn't get any uninterrupted sleep in that place. Upon our arrival we slept in old bug-infested beds, donated by colleagues to help us out.

The itchiness and rash around the waistline was a telltale sign of the infamous but common Queensland Bed Bugs as we later found out.

While we awaited the transcontinental arrival of our own furniture, we had to sleep on a blow up a mattress (after we removed the infested beds).

It would take us about a year to find our dream home on Dundowran Beach. Situated next to a nature reserve, we were surrounded by the sound of nature and could hear the waves from our bedroom.

I was in my second trimester and I had pelvic disability again so it was no fun at all. Tossing and turning, waking up from back and hip pain, Mark and I didn't get much sleep those first months. As soon as our furniture arrived things got a lot better.

I started work and my colleague was a friendly Fijian doctor. I told them I was pregnant and started working half days only.

In fact everything just seemed to fall into place for us. Mark started work at one of the local architect firms and my working environment was pleasant.

The practice had one hyperthyroid receptionist who managed the practice and also did all the ophthalmic assistant jobs. She survived on black coffee and cigarettes during the day and beers at night. Melissa was an ideal asset!

My pregnancy was totally different to the last one. My work with Angels and intuition was so deep now that I knew more. I called on my Angels. I did the right prayers. I didn't stick with fear. I was light and full of love. I called on the right energies and it was easy and light.

I found a really good Romanian obstetrician, who also trained in South Africa. Dana was amazing. She found out that I had pregnancy-induced asthma. She sent me to a really good thoracic specialist who confirmed the diagnosis. Rosemary put me on the appropriate inhalers. She was such a clever lady, she actually changed my life. This pregnancy was 1 000 times easier now that my asthma was controlled.

I saw a Bowen Specialist (a therapist who uses techniques similar to acupressure to keep your body in a natural position). Bowen Therapy is an amazingly gentle therapy started by an Australian, Mr Bowen. I was never in a wheelchair again and I kept working until the last day of the pregnancy.

Mark went straight to work at Core Architects. It was not very creative. Australian small town design is low cost and boring (unlike their contemporary architecture for the rich which is great) but he had fun. He liked his colleagues and he settled in easily.

We went out with his work mates. I made friends with my employees and nurses. These were my friends.

But mostly Mark, Matthew and I were a threesome and we did most of our things together as a family.

Before my second child was born, I worked half time. But after I took over the practice it grew very fast and I went back to working full time when Thomas was only a few months old. That is how strong and powerful I felt.

I was hired to help Dr Jamnadas but then he ended up selling the practice to me. The hospital helped me get a loan to buy it. They supported me as a guarantor.

All this went very fast. Everything was falling into place very quickly. 2008 was our family's lucky, prosperous year! The Angels were behind me and I could not fail.

The one problem was my work visa. It was an irritation when I arrived and despite all my work and hopes, this annoyance never went away. I originally got a visa to work in an area of need. But this changed. More doctors arrived in my area and it was no longer an "area of need". So after eight years and two visas my time in Australia would come to an end in 2014.

It meant that the hospital always had power over me as I could only stay in the country as long as I worked for them. So they always controlled my practice and my career. They were also very conservative, though supportive at times. They gave me permission to expand the practice but not to bring new techniques to town. I had to toe the line.

"No one else is doing it," was their slogan, "so you can't do it either."

The technical progression of my career really stagnated and fell backwards during those years in Australia. The highlight, however, was that I got to live my dreams in the sun and explore Australasia to the fullest. We toured Fiji, New Zealand, Bora-Bora and everywhere we could.

Thomas was born on 1 June 2007 and it couldn't have been more different to my first birthing experience. Everything went so smoothly and my obstetrician, Dana Moisuc, was really lovely, spiritual and understanding and the birth went like a dream. I worked up to the end of my term on half days and I was relaxed and confident.

At this stage because I had my own practice I could also control my own hours so I took a full three weeks off. I went back to work when Thomas was only three weeks old and a week later he started at a kindergarten a few miles down from my workplace. I used to drive there during my lunch break to breastfeed him. It was ten minutes by car. It was an amazing time for our young family.

My practice was flourishing, we were happy and it felt as if life was going well.

Mark's mother came to stay and help for a month when Thomas was born.

Thomas and I both got E.Coli septicemia when he was only one month old.

This can be lethal in newborns. They treated us correctly (but not in a very friendly way) in the local Hervey Bay hospital. As soon as Thomas' temperature came down after 24 hours of intravenous antibiotics, I took him home and we both finished our course of oral antibiotics in a friendly home environment. Lieve (Thomas' godmother), Veronique and I called in the healing Angels, I gave Thomas Reiki and we both recovered faster than any doctor had expected.

Mark's father had died when he was 45 from cancer. Mark had told me that many men in his family died this young. One pastor had told him that there was a curse on the family and that all the second sons would die young.

Thomas was my second son and that made me nervous.

Mark was the second son to his older brother Michael. So this conversation always weighed heavily on me. Thomas always cried when he was put to bed. He received anti reflux treatment and slept on an incline. However, because he refused to eat he didn't grow normally. He also held his tummy in pain most of the time. Mark and I took him to see the local children's specialist over and over again. Finally after three years we changed doctor and paediatrician and Thomas was send for a gastroscopy and colonoscopy. They found a very large stomach ulcer.

He got a bit better on medication but then he became so constipated he needed surgery for that too.

To this day he is still very skinny and short and he still associates food with pain. But with Thomas I am aware and will not let anything slip past me. He will get his gastroscopies regularly from the age of 18. The curse will end here!

CHAPTER 28

A time of loss

My father died before Thomas turned one.

We had never been particularly close but it had been a lucky chain of events that while awaiting the documents to start working in Australia, we had spent six months staying with him and my mom in Belgium. My dad had been loving and kind. He loved Matthew and he went to the bakery, took Matthew to see the trains and to the forest to feed the wild boars. He had been an absent father, but turned out to be a fantastic grandfather.

It turned out that he had a heart condition for years but had been hiding it. In fact, he had been ill for a long time but told no one.

I remember trying to Skype him from our dream house on the beach but the connection was always bad. I could see on the screen that he looked ill. I insisted he see a doctor. After that he didn't speak to me anymore. The doctor had told him he needed urgent heart valve replacement but my father was afraid of surgery so he decided to keep it a secret and to slowly die from heart failure, which he did.

It was just before Christmas and we were planning to fly to Belgium to see my family.

I was feeling my father's stress in my body. I knew he was not being treated well. I wanted him moved away from that rural hospital, as I knew his condition was serious. But nobody believed me. The hospital nurses I spoke to on the phone thought he was faking it.

Even my brother told me, "He's fine Veerle, he's faking it."

They only realised how sick he was when he collapsed a week later.

We got a call to say that my father was really not good. I moved our flights forward and we rushed to the airport. I felt extremely distressed and I had felt like this for days

He was moved to the academic hospital of Leuven - the same hospital where I trained and Mark would die - for emergency open-heart surgery.

We were on our way there. We had a stopover of a few hours in Malaysia. The previous days I had been very nervous as I felt my father, at the other side of the world, struggling to hold on to his life. As we arrived in Kuala Lumpur airport with its modern glass and steel terminal, a sudden peace descended over me.

"He's dead," I said to Mark.
"My father just died, I can feel it."

I could feel it in my body. The sensation of struggle in my heart and belly had been replaced by a sense of acceptance. My shoulder and jaw muscles relaxed, my heartbeat slowed down and my breathing deepened. I felt peaceful. I went from a feeling of distress to a feeling of nothingness.

After landing in Brussels, I phoned the hospital from a pay phone. They confirmed his death.

It was a very strange time. My younger brother refused to see me. He was furious about something.

I found out later that my father had told all of them on his deathbed that he was so proud of me – his daughter, a surgeon who had travelled the world. Proudest of all of them, he had said. This was too much for my brother. He was in a bad place himself and dealing with his own demons. He told me that he never wanted to see me again. And from that point he completely disappeared from my life. It even felt as if he didn't like me or want me to be happy.

My father had never in my life told me how proud he was of me. I was so touched to hear what he had said, but it was bittersweet as it meant I lost my dear brother over it and that it had come too late for me to hear him say it. The price was high.

My father's funeral was a profound experience for me. I witnessed the opening of heaven's gate as the vibration of the church bells changed the frequency of the air.

It took place in our 700 years old town church on the hill that gives my birthplace its name: Heist O/D Berg. Women had to sit at the left side of the church. My husband and two little sons were guided to the right. I felt abandoned and lonely. My heart broke as the first man I have ever loved was departing this earthly plane. His coffin was carried in by my two brothers and others.

When the two church bells started singing, the energy was so all consuming, healing my heart, and opening conversation with my father's spirit who was content. I saw that white tunnel opening right in front of me and my father's soul went up into heaven's gates with a little wave and a serene smile.

I felt divine peace in my heart. I even heard my father ask whether I wanted to come with him. "Not yet," I answered, although tempted by the beauty.

I had two small children to take care of and I realised I had now taken his place in the world of life.

Do church bells invite Angels to earth?

CHAPTER 29

Deportation looms

Thomas was just nine months when I got a letter to inform me that I could no longer stay and work in Australia unless I passed the local ophthalmology exams.

I had already passed these exams in Belgium and in South Africa and now I had to do it all over again! I was angry and frustrated. I didn't sign up for more exams when I had left my very lucrative workplace in Bruges to follow my dream in Australia! Exams are incredibly demanding as a student, but as a mom of two small kids with a busy practice they are torture.

Thomas was just under a year when I had to start studying. That was hard. I had to close the door and study for hours and hours. He used to bang on the door and I would turn him away again and again. I had to choose between studying every non-working hour of the day and spending time with my babies. Mark and I thought we had no choice as I was the breadwinner. I was thrown back to the same place. I was working in the day and studying at night.

Then I found out I was pregnant for a third time.

It wasn't a surprise. I knew it was a girl because I had planned it all. I had studied all the ways the sex of a baby could be influenced before and during conception.

I studied my own natal chart to find the best time of the year to conceive at my age as I could use all the help I could find. I found the date that the moon would be in the same position as at my own birth in the month of March. I was very aware of my regular cycle and when I would be fertile that month.

For a girl it is best to make love the three days before ovulation, because female-producing sperm survives longer. For a boy it works best to have intercourse during the three days after ovulation as the male-producing sperm swims faster (it carries less DNA and is therefore lighter).

I put my alarm on and woke Mark up in the middle of the night.

He wasn't feeling well but he did his duty.

I had summoned many Angels to help us conceive. I called on the big African Fertility Goddess. I had read the moon charts and lined that up with my astrology to get the best date to produce a daughter after two sons. This date and time had been put in my diary six months in advance. I had also starting eating an unhealthy diet of bread, meat and other acid-producing foods. The idea is that when the mother's reproductive tract has a lower pH (is more acid) the male-producing sperm has less chance to survive than their female competitors during the race to the egg they all want to fertilise.

Archangel Jophiel helped with that and I also did a meditation with the King of Elves to bring me a daughter. After Isabella was born I put gifts of shells and a pearl in the forest nearby where they hang out. Six weeks later my pregnancy test was positive.

I felt elated as I went to work that morning.

Work was even more busy than usual that day. My practice was booming but I was very stressed because of the pending exam. My practice nurse was pushing more and more patients in my room. "I need a break," I told her as I put my feet up. I felt faint.

She brought in another patient and another, against my clear order. The stress triggered an asthma attack at work and it escalated. Next thing my blood pressure skyrocketed and my heart went crazy.

I was taken to the emergency department in an ambulance. My physician admitted me to a private room and I saw a cardiac specialist.

I was told I had developed a stress-induced heart condition and I had to have urgent heart surgery the next day. I was in shock. I told him I was pregnant. He told me I was going to have to terminate.

"You can fall pregnant later," he said.
But I was 43 and I had planned this baby for so long. I shook my head and silent tears started rolling down my cheeks.

"No way," I thought as I clenched my jaw and fists, "No way, I am going to let you or anyone else kill my daughter."

I tapped into my intuition. My intuition told me that I was going to be okay. I was not going to lose this baby.

I called my psychic healer friend and she came to my bed. She confirmed my thoughts.

"Both you and this baby are going to be fine," she told me.
I knew it deep inside. I was so sure and clear.

The next day I was feeling okay and I was discharged. But I was facing a crazy situation where I was 43 and pregnant with a serious heart condition. My pelvis was finally okay, my asthma was under control but now I had a heart condition!

"I am not happy with this!"
But I had learned so much. Most of all I had learned to trust myself above all else.

I knew I had to trust myself and tackle it my way.

I found a new heart specialist in the city of Brisbane. During the pregnancy, I couldn't even take medication so I was treated with magnesium! It lowers the blood pressure and it stops muscles cramps, including the premature contractions I suffered from.

I took back my power during Isabella's pregnancy.

"This time is my time!" I told Mark, who was a bit taken aback by my newfound mothering wish.

I had always had C-Sections and he had cared for both previous babies because I had been bed-bound while recovering. This time I wanted to care for my last baby, all by myself.

My first born, Matthew, had been put in a box-bed in my room while I was strapped to the hospital bed for the first three days so I hadn't been able to touch him, cuddle him, not even when I asked the nursing staff.

This time I had an amazing obstetrician from Romania who trained in South Africa and she understood me. She let Mark stay with me when I had the epidural. I stood up for myself. I told the nurses what I wanted. I was stronger and more confident.

"This time I want my baby with me at all times," I stated.

"This time, we are doing things My Way!"

My intuition told me: This daughter is supposed to be with us and she is going to be fine. And she was: Isabella was born on 16 December 2009 with no problems at all.

But the joy was about to end as one life began, another was about to end.

CHAPTER 30
Mark goes into freefall

I sat the exams with three tiny babies in the house. I failed. The stress on me was huge.

But apart from the kids and work, Mark had changed. He had been feeling very low for months and he wanted to go home to South Africa. We had three tiny children and I had a busy practice! It was out of the question!

But it seemed that his strange behaviour was going to continue.

Mark was the backbone of our family. He always had been. He did most of the cooking. I came home and the food was on the table. It had always been like that in our relationship and he had always taken the larger share of the house duties. His company had been more flexible with work hours so he did all the school lifts. The kids went to aftercare and he got them after work at 5pm.

My hours were too irregular to be the responsible one with the children. I couldn't operate and know my children were waiting. There were lots of emergencies that came in at the last minute. Added to that I was studying almost all weekend.

But he started to feel really ill and tired.

He took a month off work. The doctor thought he had glandular fever. He slept most of time but he could not shake it.

The company he worked for was having problems and they fired him.

It was a shock. Now Mark was at home all day and very down and unhappy. Our relationship began to go downhill from then. He was staying at home, depressed and tired all the time. I was the breadwinner. He was the housekeeper.

Now he wasn't working but the strain was still huge. He couldn't handle the children and the house. I knew I needed help in the house. I got a cleaner two days a week. She then became the nanny while I had Isabella.

Our relationship was increasingly strained. He had changed. He was tired all the time and very down emotionally. We went for relationship therapy for a whole year. It went nowhere.

Every session I would ask:
"What is wrong with you?"
"I can feel something isn't right."
"Just tell me what is going on!"
"Mark, what can I do to make you happy?"
He would give me a list of jobs around the house.

He believed that parents had to do everything for their kids. I didn't believe that. I believe in hiring help, particularly with the cleaning. I could not meet his needs on this.

Something strange was going on and I could feel it. I was growing so fast in my work with Angels and intuition. I was starting to read auras and work very strongly with Angels during surgery. I was calling on healing Angels and also being advised more and more by the presence of skilled surgeons who had passed on.

But despite all of this, I was surprisingly blind to what was going on in my very own life. Because right next to me, my husband was slowly dying.

I am an intuitive! That is what I do. I operate on sick people every day. I feel and diagnose them. And yet beside me my husband was dying and I didn't know.

But in truth I felt all Mark's illnesses all along. But I got one thing wrong - I thought it was me that was sick, not him!

One day I came home from a conference of a few days and I noticed that over that short time his face had become thinner but his belly was larger. I teased him.

"Did you eat all the chocolates in the house while I was away?" I asked him.

His body odour had changed too and I thought he smelled bad. I always loved his smell but now that changed. I didn't like the way he smelled and his breath was really bad. He even complained about it. He used to eat mints and gargled Listerine mouthwash but nothing really fixed it.

He kept going back to his general practitioner. She told him his immunity was low.

"Take some vitamins and time off," she said.

"You have glandular fever," was the next diagnosis

This was when his work finally fired him. He had been off work for more than a month. Mark didn't fight them. He didn't want to be a burden for the company.

None of this rang true for me.

I asked to see his blood tests results. I saw they were highly abnormal and my colleague consulting next door confirmed this. He also advised me to send Mark to another doctor. I told Mark that night but he refused.

"I like this doctor, I am not changing," was his stubborn reply.
I called his general practitioner. She fought with me and told me she was furious I was second-guessing her!

"Are you sending him for an ultrasound of his liver?" I asked timidly.

"Who is Mark's doctor, you or me?" she yelled at me.

"You are of course. But I can clearly see from these results that Mark needs more investigations and I am just an eye specialist!"

I sent him for an ultrasound of his liver regardless. But they didn't send me the report. They sent it to the general practitioner and not me! She got the results showing metastasis and she didn't take it further. She confirmed her diagnosis of glandular fever, even though I found out later that the tests had showed extreme liver failure.

Of course it is not ethical to treat your own family so I backed off, but I begged him to see another doctor. He had the ultrasound and there were lesions on his liver. I called her again. But she said they were part of the original diagnosis.

Mark still chose to stay with her.

But I was picking up something else.

His energy was so dark and heavy that I didn't want to be near to him physically. I used to lie as far as possible from him on the bed. It was the energy of disease.

I started to have the same symptoms. My stomach was bloated and sore. I had a colonoscopy and a gastroscopy. I even went for an abdominal MRI scan. I had all the tests he should have had.

I knew there was something desperately wrong but no doctors could find out what was wrong.

Of course they couldn't! It wasn't me at all.

Mark would wake up at night with such a severe stomach pain at times that he screamed out loud. I told him I would take him to the hospital. He refused to go.

My intuition was screaming at me. I could hardly breathe for the volume of the feeling that "something was terribly wrong".

My heart condition flared up again. I ended up in intensive care twice. The cardiologist sent me to loads of tests and he brought up the heart surgery again. I wasn't keen to have eight hours of radiation with a strong family history of lymphoma.

Some of the local doctors in Hervey Bay started calling me a hypochondriac again. What I didn't realise at the time is that I am an empath – I was feeling all of Mark's symptoms at this point.

So it was crazy. I had all these physical signs and I was very ill and Mark was worried about me. But the truth was that he was feeling so bad. He just never said anything. He was in denial about the seriousness of his own ailments.

I have this tradition that I travel, not work on my birthdays. This was my 45th birthday and it had been an unpleasant, stressful year since my 44th birthday in Bora Bora, the year before. I decided to take Mark away for a surprise weekend to our favourite beach town to have surf lessons. It was the first time in a long time it would be just the two of us.

Rainbow Beach is two hour's drive south of Hervey Bay. It is a very small beach town with only half a main street. One tourist bus a week with wandering youngsters stops here for a surf lesson. It is very relaxed and quiet. Mark and I stayed there many times with our children in a modern apartment only 20 metres from the cliff down to the big sandy beach and surf waves.

This is the place where I was happiest when I was riding the waves on my body board, wearing my widest smile.

"Woohoo, did you see that?" I would scream to Mark and later to Matthew. I felt exhilarated flying over the water at high speed. The sand stuck to my hair. The salty sea water rinsed my sinuses. The sun tanned my arms and legs, not covered by the board shorts and the sun shirt.

This Australian beach outfit helps to protect your skin against the scorching sun rays and the sea sand.

"That was a nine out of ten," I would agree with Matthew, picking up my pink board out of the waves. I carried it high under my right arm as I strode back into the crashing waves. This was heaven to me. I had more or less overcome my fear of drowning, since South Africa - but still avoided rip curls.

I had booked this weekend away so we would be able to relax and enjoy some adult time for a change.

Mark had been complaining that he was tired and didn't want to watch the children anymore, and that he felt unloved by me. I thought that the solution for all three of these problems would be found in one chilled-out, childfree weekend.

As soon as we arrived in Rainbow Beach, we checked in for the surf lessons. We were an hour early so Mark suggested we go to the best coffee shop in Main Street (there were two) as our favourite spiritual pizza restaurant, which had mantra- decorated walls, had closed down.

He looked uptight, pale and tired. His face had become very drawn, and his cheeks were hollow. His potbelly was still there, which was weird and looked unnatural on such a lean man.

"What is wrong, Mark?" I asked, as he sat down in front of me staring down at his hands. "Can you lighten up, please? We finally have some time for us."

"Veerle, we need to talk."

My heart dropped into my sandals.

The last time, I heard that sentence delivered in that way was when Johan broke up with me more than 15 years earlier.

I felt nauseous and felt goose bumps. No, this can't really be happening, not now!

I stared outwardly calm and intense at my soulmate Mark, the father of our three small children, my best friend and the only family I had on this continent.

"I am leaving you. I want to move out of the house into my own apartment. I am tired of taking caring of you and the kids and not getting any appreciation in return," he added. He looked very angry. I had never seen Mark like this before. The enormous love he had for me before had turned into hate.

I was reeling.

"Please don't do this now, I know it's tough. We have small kids and I have to prioritise my second and last chance to get through this exam. This is not the right time to leave me," I begged him. "I can't cope without you!"

"WE need you!" I tried.

"Things will go back to normal soon," I promised as tears started rolling over my cheeks.

"I can't manage the kids, a practice and a huge exam, without you," I started crying. Please, don't leave me, not now. I need you. I can't cope without you."

His face remained cold as my warm tears ran down my cheeks and started dripping of my chin. My nose also started leaking but I just sobbed, I didn't care what the strangers around us were thinking. My life, as I knew it, had just ended.

"I want to see if I feel better when I am not with you."

Mark didn't budge. He kept on staring at me with hate in his eyes, tension in his jaw and clenched fists.

"After I pass the exam, I will have more time for you and the children and we can become residents and we are going to be fine. Our future together in Australia will be wonderful," I argued.

"Veerle I am tired."

"I want out."

"I don't want to do this anymore."

"You don't feel like kissing me. "

"I don't feel loved by you anymore."

"Tired. Tired. Tired."

"But what about the children?" I asked flabbergasted.

"We can take those fifty-fifty," he answered quickly. This was already clear in his head.

"But I have to study for the exam," I sobbed.

"That is not my problem", he replied. "I have never wanted to live in Australia anyways. I only came here for you. It was your dream, not mine."

"Where would you like to live then?"

"You know I liked our time in Belgium the most. I can get an architect job there with my previous colleagues. I am looking for jobs in the UK too." He was hard and cold. He had made up his mind. There was no turning back.

I didn't end up surfing in the waves. After the one-hour practice on the beach, my right shoulder was so sore that I couldn't paddle through the high waves anymore.

I was in shock. Of course, now I have the benefit of hindsight and I can see the entire episode in context. I know now that this was his way out. On a soul and a spiritual level I now know that he was preparing me for the fact that he was leaving the children, his life and me soon.

And in a practical way it started to prepare myself to live without him. Even though it was a huge shock I started to ready myself for him leaving me. It was something I had never thought about. I thought that there was no way I could live without him. But for the first time I had to contemplate this happening as a reality. I just didn't realise how fast he would leave me, or how much we would still have him around.

CHAPTER 31

The first time he died

Three months later we went for a family holiday to Belgium. We had planned a family trip to Belgium with the whole family ages ago. It was an annual thing we did and the trip usually follows a similar pattern. Mark takes care of the children on the plane as I have had so many health issues for so long and I would nap or study. This was the first time ever he walked onto the plane, sat on an empty seat away from the kids and me and slept the entire flight. All my senses were on high alert and screaming: "Something is seriously wrong!"

We landed and hired a taxi to take us to my mum's house. We went to buy food but Mark had problems even walking the 100 metres to the city centre to shop. Every day he got worse.

I noticed he was eating less and less but his belly got bigger and bigger by the day. It was distended and noticeable through his clothing. He was in pain.

About two days after we arrived we were going to visit my mom at the seaside town. I had made a routine appointment with a really good dermatologist who we used every year to examine our skin. Mark has pale skin with red hair and was very sun sensitive. Every year he had a few sunspots to freeze off.

But as we were driving to her Mark was in serious pain. He was doubled over. This was not normal at all!

We arrived at the surgery and he could hardly even walk in. When she saw us she looked alarmed. He managed to sit during the session as she burned off the lesions. But in the middle of the session he had an attack of what I can only call severe pain. He was doubled over in agony and screaming

She told me to get him to the hospital, and fast.

I got him in the car and drove. I dragged him into the empty emergency department of a small regional hospital in Flanders on a hot Saturday afternoon. There was nobody on the streets. The place was deserted.

There was nobody around. I had to walk around calling out for help. Eventually I found some staff sitting cooling off in a back room.

"Yeah, what's wrong?"

A nurse eventually poked her head out.

"I need someone to look at my husband. He is in serious pain. I am a doctor. Please help."

Eventually some of the emergency staff came and attended to Mark.

They put him on a stretcher, asked us some questions and took a medical history. The nurse ran some blood tests and then they took him for a CT scan.

We weren't sent home. We weren't told to come back weeks later for tests as would happen in most hospitals. They did everything in a few minutes right there and then.

We sat waiting. An hour later the physician on call came back with the diagnosis.

It was delivered quickly, just one hour after we had walked in.

Mark had stomach cancer. It was terminal and it had spread to his liver, lungs and brain.

This was not what we had expected. But on another level it was a strange feeling of relief that we finally knew. I had felt this coming for so long.

As the doctor gave us the diagnosis, I was overcome with nausea. I felt dizzy. I wanted to escape the hard reality that I was being confronted with. For a year I had felt anxiety and fear. I had thought I was going to die. I had got so many messages but I hadn't heard them.

Finally I knew why all these things were happening.

I also knew without a doubt that it was the beginning of the end.

After delivering the news that Mark was going to die soon they sent us home.

They discharged Mark but they wanted him to come back on the Monday for a biopsy of the tumour. In the meantime I got on the phone. I called a friend who was a professor in Leuven. He organised for Mark to have the gastroscopy on the next Monday in Gasthuisberg University Hospital, which was closer to where we were staying.

On Monday we arrived for the gastroscopy in Leuven. I watched the entire procedure. The tumour in his stomach was huge and bleeding. The doctors told us that it was too big to operate on.

But some good news came back in the biopsy. It was the type that would respond well to chemotherapy. This was a relief and Mark showed signs of hope.

Since the diagnosis that weekend Mark had never showed any real emotions. He was stoic. He seemed to accept the diagnosis as if he had known it all along – or expected it.

Things were happening so fast. It was a week from diagnosis to when he was due to start chemotherapy and that week was an intense one.

For the first time in a long time the two of us spoke from the heart.

I now understood why he had been so mean and grumpy for so long. I told him I loved him so much. He was so thankful that I loved him still.

It was a week from diagnosis to chemo. But I had a feeling that this was not going to be a long story. Everybody else was upbeat and positive, but I knew how fast it would go. I was the only one. I asked my brother to come and film Mark with his children for one last time. But my family said I was being crazy. "Relax! It is not that quick," they told me: "He won't be gone that fast."

But I was right. A month later he was gone. Luckily I took some photos of him in the garden with the kids. It was a lovely warm summer day and I made sure to get some records of him for his children.

His birthday was on the 21 June 2012 and he was turning 46. A friend came from Holland to have lunch with us. I told our friends about the diagnosis and asked them to come for a meal before his chemo. We all had a meal with about ten friends and we had fun and laughed. I even joked and said:

"This is like the last supper."

And it was.

The next day he went in to have his first chemotherapy session. He was admitted to a two-bed room in the oncology ward.

In the bed next to him was a man who had lived with stomach cancer for a year. Mark also met an older man who had had it for five years and another who had survived for two years. This all seemed to boost his confidence. Mark liked chatting to these men and got support. He was optimistic as they were still alive. One became a good friend. Mark stayed in the hospital for a few days while he received the first chemo treatment.

Mark and I were really close over this week. It was as if we were clinging to each other and the love we remembered having. I understood why I had been the way I was.

Everything became clear to me. Why I couldn't touch him or kiss him or have sex with him. I was feeling the disease. I understood his moods and his terrible tiredness that had weighed on our family for so long. It all meant nothing.

I forgave him and we were close and loving. I wanted to believe that there was hope to keep him alive for a few years. I was confident.

But my gut intuition had told me he would be dead in a month. I kept that to myself now.

I knew my job now was to keep his spirits up.

It was a stressful time. Our children and I didn't have anywhere to stay in the city where Mark was admitted into Gasthuisberg Hospital in Leuven, the number one university hospital in Belgium (ranked number 63 worldwide).

It was there that I had done my medical training. I had lived there, in a small student room, for several years and I knew the place well. It is the city where my second brother lived. Naturally I called my brother and asked if I could stay with him. He agreed so I moved in with my three tiny children for a few days.

We had planned to go to the Belgian seaside for Mark to recover after his first dose of chemotherapy. I could take our children to the beach while he had a quiet space in which to rest.

The plan was that he would rest and recover and then we would go back a month later for the next dose of chemo.

I was having another battle. This time it was with the health insurance cover we had from Australia. Luckily Mark had bought travel insurance from Australia that included medical cover. It was going to cover the medical costs. They wanted Mark to fly back to Australia to complete his treatment. However his local doctors said: "There is no way he can fly!"

"He may bleed to death on the plane," one said.

His tumour was huge and bleeding internally and he was in a very serious condition.

After the first chemo treatment Mark became weaker every day. The first day in Knokke we had breakfast in a typical Belgian bakery and we walked through the town, window shopping, looking at art and watching our children drive go karts on the wide Esplanade. Mark chose his favourite fresh ice cream from The Post before resting in the comfortable cushioned benches at the Zoute Beach Bar where we watched our children frolic happily in the sand and on the slide. It was early evening when Mark decided to go to bed in the seaside apartment. He would not leave that bed much after.

On Day Two he was relatively okay and we even had a visitor – it was one of his best South African friends who had relocated to the Netherlands with her husband. I gave them some space by taking the children to one of the play parks on the beach. When I came back both Mark and his friend were very sad and emotional. They hugged for the last time.

On Day Three, a friend who was a doctor friend of mine visited and our professor friend came with his young family too. My older brother and his family also came to see us. Mark even sat at the table with us while the big group of visitors finished all the bread rolls with ham and cheese. Mark sat up to chat to the guests for a bit and then he went back to bed. I could see he was suffering but he was stoic and always put others before himself. So he remained his polite attentive self the day before he died for the first time.

Mark was very weak and this time I had noticed that Mark's attitude had changed. He was saying farewell to friends and people who came to see him.

On Day Four, his condition had deteriorated and he was in excruciating abdominal pain that was no longer suppressed by the extra pain medication prescribed by the hospital when I had consulted them daily about his deteriorating condition. Even though I had never been with anyone who had chemo, I didn't think this was normal. He was in agony and throwing up.

I called the hospital every day asking the registrar on call, "Is this normal?"

"Just give him some more codeine," she answered.

"Yes," they told me, "it is normal."

But he got worse and worse.

On the fourth day and after countless frantic calls to his doctors I called again.

"This is not normal!" I said panicky to the head nurse of the oncology department, who answered the phone for the first time.

"Bring him into emergency immediately," was his answer.

My family was not there to support me.

I called my oldest friend, Myriam, who came and took Mark and I to hospital. Another friend and his young family took our children for the day. Lieve stayed behind to pack up all our gear from the seaside apartment.

Mark was in such a bad state that he couldn't even sit up. His life force was leaving him, straight in front of my eyes. Some students and registrars came. Our professor friend came to have a look. Then the treating oncologist came.

They took one look. "Organ failure," they said.

They put him on a stretcher with tubes everywhere. They put him straight on life support.

They sent me off. They said:

"It is too awful to watch."

"You have to go!"

Another doctor, who was completely unknown to me, stopped me on the way out of the emergency department.

"Veerle," she said, "I don't think he is going to survive the night."

"Don't go too far," she insisted.

"I have seen this before; I know what I am talking about"

Those words were a huge shock to me.

Mark was successfully revived that night but was kept in an artificial coma.

He ended up in intensive care on life support for close to two weeks on dialysis and in renal failure. His cancer too far advanced for surgery and he was too weak to consider any further chemo. They kept him in an induced coma.

I went home that night and left him in their hands. I prayed that the Angels would somehow make Mark miraculously better.

In my crisis, my Angels were all around me. Since the diagnosis in the little country hospital, I had felt them everywhere. I was in such a high vibration, all the time that I was surrounded by them.

I didn't sleep. I didn't eat. I just called on them the whole time. I prayed a lot. I asked the Angels to be with me. I also had very vivid dreams.

The long week Mark was in a coma they carried me through the pain and loss.

One night I woke in the middle of the night and someone was hovering over me. I knew it was Mark's astral body coming to visit me.

The next day they called me into the hospital early. In the middle of the night Mark had started haemorrhaging again. They gave him 20 litres of blood and resuscitated him. That night he had died and been revived for the very last time. I think it was his spirit body visiting me in the night as he left his body.

The doctor told me that they would not resuscitate him another time.

"We know his diagnosis, and it is just a matter of time. Do you understand?"

"Yes," I said. "No!" I wanted to scream.

Family and friends had taken our three little children out for a day at a time each. Officially, children were not allowed in the intensive care unit.

Seeing the fast decline their father was making, the hospital staff made an exception to the rule, Belgian style, and allowed our children to visit their father every day, even while he was in a coma.

Healthcare is so good in Belgium. We even got our own psychologist at that hospital. There was a social worker that helped us to find a place to stay nearby. I ended hiring a stranger I found in the newspaper to help me with the children. They allowed them to come to ICU even when he had tubes in. She also advised me to take photos of Mark with our children, even while he was on artificial life support. The psychologist said: "They must see their father otherwise they will get so angry when they are older that you took that opportunity away from them." They were so young. Isabella was only two years old.

We were lucky we were in Belgium – it was divine intervention. In Australia I would have had neither family nor friends nor this excellent, caring level of healthcare, to support us like this.

The hospital was so good and accommodating to us. I could eat there. I ended up sleeping there most nights. They were good people who made a horrible experience a bit easier.

I had a cousin who was 18 who helped me with the children. I found a nice house with furniture. We moved in for a few weeks. That was a big blessing. The owner felt sorry for us and said he would be happy to get paid later by our insurance.

I tried to spend as much time as possible by Mark's side and raced back to the house only for a bath and to sleep. We were all under extreme stress and my brother was taking on a lot of it.

During the afternoon I received a phone call from him. He told me he would prefer it if I moved to my mother's house as it was too difficult for him and his family to have us all there.

My older brother was on holiday in the United States and as soon as he came back he was a huge support. His daughters played with the children for a few days. They did what they could.

My mother came back home from her seaside convalescence, after she had knee surgery for a fractured kneecap. But she was no real help on any level, least of all on an emotional one. She had a broken leg and was sleeping in the living room on a hospital bed. My mother only gave me one piece of advice when she found out Mark was going to die.... She put her hands on my shoulders and looked me straight in the eyes.

"You think it is bad now but it is going to be a lot worse later."

I think I knew then that there was something wrong with her.. and that I was not going to be like her. She was never a proud mother. She never complimented me. She was never kind.

"She is nobody special," she used to say about me.

But I was something special. No more special than any other child but every child of God deserves love and respect.

Even Mark didn't want her to visit him.

One night I had an allergic reaction and my skin broke out in blisters. I called my uncle's wife who was a nurse, and asked her to take me to the closest emergency department. She told me she could not and advised me to call the doctor on call. Everyone was under great strain.

My mother was there, undermining me as usual.

"Do you really think you need this!" she said.

I had to use my doctor voice and say, "Listen! Who is the doctor here?'

There was an elderly doctor on call. He came to my home at 1am and examined me. He had all the necessary medication with him, as I needed to take steroids urgently.

But he did more than give me medicine. He gave me the attention I desperately needed. This busy man sat with me for an hour, in the dead of night, and listened to me. He calmed me down and talked to me in a way my family was not able to. He saved my sanity that night.

I have found that Angels come in all forms and sometimes in the form of a stranger.

CHAPTER 32
Angels hold me

It was at this time I knew my Angels were all around. They never left my side. If they left at night I called them back the next day. Every day before I went into the hospital I prayed. Please give me the strength to get through another day.

I had to get through the abandonment. My family failed me. Mark was dying. I had nobody to count on. My father had died and he had been my support until I found Mark. I felt so alone and abandoned. The only thing that pulled me through was the Angels.

Every day I had to walk from the hospital rooftop parking to Mark's

ICU (Intensive Care Unit) room. I called for my Angels and I could feel their wings around me like a warm blanket holding me. I felt soothed. I download energy from them. I see it as colour. With a pipe of white light I rinse out my body from all the darkness I have collected, with the help of Archangel Michael.

I connect with the earth and pull energy up my legs into my body to keep on walking and keep on going despite of the sleep deprivation and lack of nutritional intake (lack of food). The hurt and stress made me seriously anorexic.

I usually do that every day, but at this time I was doing it a few times a day.

When I am really in distress I call Archangel Michael. I called on him most days.

Mark had just a month between his diagnosis that day in that tiny clinic and dying. For two of those weeks he was in a coma on life support.

When it was clear there was no hope, they woke him up for the last week so he could consciously say goodbye to his family.

When they woke him they moved him out of intensive to palliative care to room 13. My heart sank. There was no hope left.

My sister in law had seen her aunt and a friend die from cancer in that room. “They never come out.” She shook her head in despair.

Mark’s mother had flown out to see him and she had spent a few days by his side. It was great to have her there as it took a bit of the pressure off me.

Mark was stoic. He didn’t want to cause his mother in pain.

“When are you going?” he asked her every day. He didn’t really want anyone around him except me.

She had been there a few days and was due to fly back to South Africa that night. I had left him alone with his mom and an older cousin so they could have private time with him to say goodbye on their last day.

I took the day off hospital duty and took the kids to the Antwerp Zoo for the day.

I returned to the hospital late in the evening. Mark’s mom said goodbye to us and I walked her to the elevator. As I walked back and into his room he started losing blood..

It was like he had been holding it in all day. It was litres and litres of blood just pouring out of his mouth. I was catching it in kidney-shaped containers.

This was the end they had warned me about. Mark had signed papers that told the hospital not to intervene when it came to this.

But at the end, Mark wasn’t ready to die.

“I need intervention! I don’t care what we agreed. I need a blood transfusion. Now! ” He panicked.

I too was holding on to hope.

But I could see this was the end. I tried to calm him, even though I desperately wanted him to survive too.

The palliative head nurse told him: "You need to let go now. This is what is going to happen. You said you were ready and you agreed with the doctors. They have explained why they would not give you a transfusion again."

But he was scared. He didn't want to hear that.

"Please help me," he said.

It was Friday night. I was freaking out. I ran out of the corridor and found the palliative doctor on call.

"Please help him," I begged.

"Please, he is not ready to die. Can you send him back to ICU?"

It caused a big drama in the hospital, as this was against the rules and agreements. Doctors were all called in and there was a lot of arguing and fighting.

It took hours of stress and fighting to get Mark transferred via the emergency department back to the intensive care unit (ICU). This was circumventing the rules: ICU is to help people survive; it is not a place where patients are sent to die.

In the meantime I stood there beside him, catching the blood coming out of his mouth and wiping his face and holding his hand. The whole time I was talking to him and trying to calm and love him.

"You are such a good father and a good husband," I told him again and again. I wanted him to feel appreciated and love. But it got him agitated. He got angry with me.

"Why do you keep on staying that," he shouted. "Stop saying that."

I called his mom who was on her way to the airport and told her what was going on.

"Do you want to come back and be with him?" I asked. I was hoping she would. Even though he hadn't wanted her there, I was so scared of being alone as he died.

But she said no. She didn't want to come back and watch her son die.

She got on the plane and left that night.

I stayed with him all night.

The staff told me that they would not give him a transfusion but they would move him to high care.

The staff at ICU said, "He is in the dying process now. You should leave. He doesn't even know you are here."

They told me that it was going to get ugly and the blood would start coming out everywhere.

"We would rather you leave and we handle it from here."

I refused.

"Call someone to come support you," the professional hospital staff told me, outside of Mark's ICU room.

"You can't go through this alone," the female hospital pastor whispered.

"You should go home," the young registrar told me." This is not gonna be pretty, I have seen this before."

"I can't leave him alone now," I answered.

"I can't leave him alone in his darkest moment," I added. "I am a doctor, I have seen death and I can handle it."

I knew I couldn't count on my family for support.

I was all alone. Both families had taken off and left me here. I started calling my friends but it was very late at night and nobody answered the phone.

We were utterly alone and I was very aware of the significance and permanence of Mark's dying process. I did my best to be loving and caring.

I felt so terribly alone. Mark had been my support for 15 years. He was my guy. He had been my family, my best friend, lover, pillar and support. I couldn't count on anyone else. Earlier that day Mark had taught me how to do Internet banking, as I didn't even know how to do that. He gave me all the passwords and showed me how to pay the bills. It was a struggle. He had always done everything for me. He had run our whole life and I had just worked and made the money.

Slowly during the night he just slipped away.

After 20 hours of horror Mark lost consciousness and all oral communication was lost. I was talking to a plant. It was the first step of letting go as all connection with him was lost. It was the end.

The whole night I sat by him trying to call any form of support. I just needed to hear a friendly voice. The only friends who answered were in Australia as they were awake.

Finally out of desperation I called my insurance company. I held on at the call centre and then when I got through I asked what forms they needed. It was perhaps an odd call to make but my mind was doing odd things. I also knew that there was certain paperwork they would need and I wanted to know what it was.

I had sat for so many hours all alone. The person at the end of the phone was nasty to me.

"How dare you," they said. "How dare you try and get his money before he is dead?"

Even they turned away from me. It was truly my darkest hour.

I was still in my bright summer dress that I had worn on the day that I took our children to the zoo. I remember walking into the hospital smelling of sunshine and then I was hit with the smell of fear and death.

I stank of fear and death now. That dress stank so much that no amount of washing could ever clean it.

But I could not leave him to wash. My beloved husband could go at any time.

It was almost morning and I was exhausted. I knew I couldn't save him. I could not pray for him to live and I was so shattered from watching his horrible death and suffering.

I went to find a nurse.

"How long will it take for him to die?" I asked.

The doctors were honest with me.

"If he wants to hold on, it can go on for days still," they told me.

"Is there any hope at all?"

"None."

Then they asked me if I wanted it to go faster.

"Please," I said.

They gave him some extra morphine and he was calmer. And an hour later he was dead.

I had been all alone with Mark going through his dying process in intensive care for the last 24 hours. I had been the one wiping the blood from his mouth after he spat it in a recycled cardboard bowl. I was the one holding his hand, whispering words of love and courage while his life energy was leaking out of him.

But as he died the room was full of Angels and spirits around him.

My dear husband's heart stopped beating and a group of doctors stood by and noted down the time of death.

I was holding onto his hand the entire time. He was still warm when they called his death and noted it. They wanted me to leave the room. Our professor friend came into the room as I started to cry.

I asked him to hug me. He was very stiff and formal but he held me and walked me out of the room. He knew Mark and me very well. He and his wife had been present at our wedding ten years earlier. The intensive care staff shut me out of the room and closed the door and that was the last time I ever saw my beloved husband.

CHAPTER 33

All alone

I had lost my soulmate, best friend, travel companion and father of our three children. The pain was all consuming. It tore apart every cell in my body, aura and soul. At least, that is how I experienced it.

It is really hard to put to words the extent of the pain. For 15 years I had shared my heart, body and soul with The One. Then he was gone. Gone was that constant presence of another caring, reliable, and strong human that loved me and cared for me.

My mom was little support.

"It feels bad today and it will only get worse!" she told me. Nice one, mum! No wonder Mark refused to see you at his deathbed. He knew.

My friends were my lifelines and I was lucky to have good ones. They got me home from the hospital that day and guided me through the next few days.

Mark had clearly stated he wanted to be cremated.

"I want you to keep my ashes in your bedroom so I can see you naked," he had instructed me cheekily.

My oldest friend Myriam came to the rescue: she personally knew a mortuary owner. She contacted him and communicated the details and date of the funeral, the preferred priest (who was on holiday), and the church (where Isabella had been baptised less than two years earlier). The funeral invitations were in Mark's favourite colour of yellow and with matching balloons.

I spend a day sobbing at home with my doctor friends who lived near. While our five young children played together in their pool and in the house, I went through Mark's iPhone listening to his favourite songs to construct a playlist of appropriate songs to play during the ceremony. I also requested that no one would wear the most depressing colour: black. Of course my mother did exactly that!

The day of the funeral, after Mark's urn was returned to us, all the guests (my friends and family) were seated in the little church in a square formation around the Baptist font. The priest mentioned that he had baptised Isabella there not so long ago and now God had taken another soul in turn. And so the wheel of Life and Death keeps spinning…

I held both my boys, who started sobbing from the sadness in the air, close to me. Isabella was not really aware of the permanence of her father's absence yet. She was composed and was seated next to her godmother, my friend Myriam, who had also organised the snacks and drinks afterwards. It is a Belgian custom to feed your guests well before they travel back home from a funeral.

CHAPTER 34
A long way home

My grandmother and mother were both strong independent women. I knew I had their genes inside me.

They survived a world war by being innovative and fearless but clever (it does sound a lot like me, no wonder we argued so much). My grandmother smuggled legs of ham on the tram and train, past the invaders, under her coat. She hid them by pretending she had a pregnant belly.

My female ancestors both attained a profession, were self-employed and the bosses at home.

My mother's dream was to get a university degree but that didn't happen easily for women of her generation. Instead she and my father both got jobs and gave their earnings to their parents. That was the way it was done those days.

I am very grateful that I was born in the late 1960s in a wealthy, safe, stable western country. Having lived, worked and travelled all over the world, I consider myself very lucky indeed. My country's government used my parent's tax money wisely for social care and free healthcare for all. I was spoiled with choice of free schooling and universities. Even my medical studies were sponsored by the state. They knew that the strength of the future economy would lie in its population's brainpower and they were right!

My particular upbringing might not have prepared me well for marriage but it has served me well to cope in times of hardship.

And this was the hardest of times.

I was alone in a foreign country with three small children. I had to fight for my professional life in Australia again. I had to survive without Mark.

At first, Lieve came back with me to help. She stayed a month before she went home but I couldn't cope. I was looking after the children, getting them to school and back, work and housework. I wasn't coping. There weren't enough hours in the day. I hardly got any sleep. A month later I hired a German au pair via an online website. She arrived a few weeks later and she helped with the children.

I had to learn how to do everything Mark had done. I had to learn how to pay the bills online, do the household chores (I had never even used the washing machine before) and do all the legal stuff. I had a solicitor so there was a will and life insurance in place but my life was shattered.

And at the same time my medical practice had almost been destroyed. When I got back I found out that in the eight weeks I had been away my competitive colleagues had tried to poach all my patients.

This was the second time this had happened. The last time was when I went to bury my father and I was away for only three weeks. A letter had been sent by a referring doctor that he was taking over all my patients. He had also told all my faithful patients: "She has left and is never coming back!" Such blatant lies!

Medicine is a competitive business in Australia.

That time I hadn't been away long enough to suffer too badly. But this time I lost a lot. All my patients had been referred out to other doctors. Even my staff had thought I was not coming back. This was even though they had been paid and had continued work in my practise … but it seems they were busy moving all my patients to other doctors.

So after burying my husband I had to fight for my professional life.

I went to work every day but had no patients.

I had to spend time visiting the local general practitioners to tell them that I was back and to ask for work. I was struggling and also travelled out of town. I put advertisements in the newspapers. It was as if I had to start all over again. So I did just that.

The positive side of having no patients to see to was that I had a lot of free time. Every morning I performed a spiritual routine until 10am. This is where the techniques that I had built into my life helped me. During my daily beach run I connected to Christ energy from my heart. I grounded myself by visualizing energy roots from the soles of my feet to the centre of the earth, to give me strength for the day. I imagined a pink cloud around my workplace so that only someone with love energy could enter.

Angels were already an everyday part of my life by now. I had lived and worked with them for so long that my entire life ran on intuition and trust.

They always brought the right people into my life, at exactly the right time.

The nurse at my practice was an earthy and practical Taurus who was a practising Catholic. She had a deep, honest faith. My receptionist, Emma, was a beautiful young spiritual woman who was connected with Angels and sensitive to energies.

I was working very hard with the help of Angels. At night I called on them for my own healing. They helped me heal my broken heart. I lived from day to day and they got me through.

But I also had to put in the hard slog to build my practice back up.

I was working so hard I had three hours of sleep a night. But I did it!

So here I was using all the magic that I had collected during my life. In Belgium I was called a witch but this didn't stop my path. I worked with Angels and I started to invite them more and more into my practice. I started working more and more with love. That was my mission. I wasn't a doctor who worked for the money or for fame. I surrounded myself and my practice with love. That was the only way I would work.

And it did work.

In six months I paid off my debts and I had again built up my practice.

I had just got on my feet financially when the next challenge came.

The work visa situation reared its ugly head again. I had to pass another Australian exam. I had been living in Australia for eight years.

They told me I had to pass the same exams as a new graduate student.

I had written the exam the first time when I found out that I was pregnant with Bella. I had a heart problem and had to have urgent surgery but instead I sat the two-day test. My score was just under the curve.

Registrars in Training get intensively groomed on how to pass this exam. I needed to know what was in the exam to pass. But to do this I needed to spend time Brisbane.

I flew to Brisbane at least twice a month to try and get access to the registrar's study material so I would know how to prepare.

This was now the fourth set of exams I had to write. I had written Belgium exams, South African exams, and the Australian ones once already.

It was very tough. I was a single working mum with a private practise. Besides my work as a specialist, I had three small children and had to find time and energy to study on top of all that. The exam is a long and intense one. It consists of two days of written exams and two days of practical tests.

They are extensive and thorough. I had already done this in South Africa and passed easily. But there I had support and access to the training for the exams. But in competitive Australia they denied me a fair chance. "We don't want you here, you are not one of the registrars in training," the organiser told me to my face. Once I flew to Melbourne to share in the training for a few days and the registrars made me sit in front of the wrong meeting room for hours while they had moved their training to another room. Doctors in Australia are trained to be competitive. Exams. You don't just have to do well; you HAVE to beat the others to make it. Only a few foreign doctors make it. If you are Australian you get ten attempts at the exam, but I only got two.

I had to pass the exam before my work visa expired. It was due to expire in October 2014. So in January 2014 I took the College exam for a second time.

CHAPTER 35

The email bomb

My practice was booming. I was almost back to the largest practice in the town and I was fully booked. I had written the exams and hadn't heard back from the Royal Australian College of Ophthalmology (RANZCO) .

It was six months later that I arrived at work one morning when my receptionist asked an unusually normal question.

"Did you check your email this morning?"

"No," I smiled, still on a high from my morning running meditation. Angels had surrounded me.

"Everything is going to work out just fine," they'd whispered.

But both my staff members had the energy of doom.

I raced to my computer and checked my mail. There it was. An email that basically said: "You are useless, drop all your work, close your practice, and send all your patients home, you can't work here anymore.

What is actually said was:

"You have been deemed non-comparable and cannot practice medicine in Australia anymore."

Non-comparable. Which meant I didn't measure up to the 30-year-olds coming straight out of university. That was the term they used!

Now I have many personal weaknesses (after all I am only human), but I do know I am an extremely competent and experienced surgeon.

The only problem is that I never had access to their exam-training program and was asked to sit exams without the preparation their own students get.

But in reality, writing a good exam does not make a good doctor. There are some doctors, who can study hard and write exams really well, but then they have to deliver a baby and they pull a woman's perineum and tear it apart. So there is a difference between writing an exam and being an effective doctor.

I realised then that they never wanted me to make it. They didn't want more foreign doctors. They wanted Australians to get all the work so my appeal was doomed from the start.

My work visa was still valid till October. I appealed the decision.

My neighbours started a petition. My patients collected 3 000 signatures demanding I stay. The story was on the front page of the national newspaper and on the 6 o'clock TV news. Politicians were involved.

The mayor came to visit me and see what was going on.

An extract from the Fraser Coast Chronicle read:

HERVEY BAY EYE DOCTOR AND HER CHILDREN FACING DEPORTATION

A DUNDOWRAN BEACH mum and her children are facing deportation unless she can retake a test that will allow her family to stay in the country.

Veerle Van Tricht, an eye specialist who came to Australia from Belgium more than seven years ago, was operating her own business, Fraser Coast Eye Specialists, when she was informed she would need to pass a test with the Royal Australian and New Zealand College of Ophthalmologists to be able to continue practicing.

Dr Van Tricht failed the exam, leaving both herself and her three children, two of whom were born in Australia, exposed to the possibility of deportation.

Dr Van Tricht said the college did not allow her to participate in any training before the test, which had hampered her ability to pass the exam.

Avril Cronk, general manager of community relations and congress for RANZCO, said the college could not comment on an individual's performance or experience with the process.

But she said a specialist who was an international medical graduate who wishes to be registered as a specialist ophthalmologist in Australia can apply for assessment through RANZCO.

Ms Cronk said RANZCO was required by the Australian Medical Board, as the registering authority, to determine the level of comparability with the individual's training, qualifications and experience with those training and qualified in Australia.

She said depending of the level of comparability, the person may be required to undertake peer review, further training or examinations.

Dr Van Tricht, who has 20 years of experience as an eye specialist, said she was hoping RANZCO might be able to offer her training prior to the exam that will leave her better able to pass it.

"Without preparation, passing the exam would be virtually impossible," she said.

Her children were distressed at the thought of leaving Australia as it was the only home they had ever known, Dr Van Tricht said.

Her children do not speak Dutch or French, the two main languages of Belgium, and while Dr Van Tricht could get work in any number of countries, she wants her family to remain in Australia.

The family is surviving by living on the life insurance Dr Van Tricht received when her husband died of cancer a few years ago and all she wants to do is go back to work.

She said it had been her dream to work in Australia since she was a child.

When operating her practice, Dr Van Tricht had 11 000 patients on her books and she was seeing people with many eye problems that are in desperate need of treatment on the Fraser Coast, such as cataracts and macular degeneration.

She said she knows her abilities are needed on the Fraser Coast and she would not want to be anywhere else.

But it all amounted to nothing.

The Health Minister replied with the statement, "I have no power."

It was a strange time for me. Years of work and dedication had ended in this.

I was a widow and alone, but fighting to stay in a country that didn't want me.

I had a lot of money invested in my practice, and in my career. And for this reason I fought for my survival.

The unfair enforced loss of my practice, my home, and my children's homeland felt devastating for all of us.

It didn't make sense to anyone but to those behind the scenes. I was finding out that Australia didn't want foreigners taking over jobs forever. A short time was accepted but not for life. Even before my arrival, RANZCO, the Royal Australian and New Zealand College of Ophthalmology had put my application on hold for six months in order to change the rules to let some foreigners in without exams. Then they changed the rules again to make it extra hard for me.

The first professional meeting I ever went to in Brisbane (I had to travel eight hours by car to go to these educational events), I introduced myself to the first doctor who arrived.

"Are you the new Doctor Patel?" the smiling, balding man said ironically.

"I am Dr Van Tricht! Whom are you talking about?" I replied, confused.

"Patel is the local Doctor Death. He killed more than 30 patients and lied about his qualifications," was his answer before he turned his back on me.

I was stunned.

So there I stood. After eight years of living and building a practice in this rural area, I was going to have to pack up my life, leave my business and start a new life somewhere else.

And so my next journey began again.

Even though my Australian childhood dream of being a Flying Doctor had lasted only eight years, I was enriched and wiser because of this experience.

I was finally free from eight years of scrutiny that had put my health, my relationship with Mark and with my children, under a lot of pressure.
I pondered how I had survived this extended period of stress. But I knew the hard times had forced me deeper into my own healing practice.

I had begun to collect all the conventional and alternative forms of healing I had used to keep me going under this very heavy load.

I knew I had to trust that my life was taking me in a new direction for a reason. I know now that it was necessary for me to be taken out of a hard time of my life, and a hard place, into a softer landing.

Even my exit from Australia was hard.

On the last hour of my stay in Australia, I was at a conference that ran late. I rushed in a taxi to meet my three children and their nanny at the airport. But I was stopped at check-in and told that we had overstayed our visa by a few hours.

I called on the immigration Angels, swallowed my pride and had to buy five more tickets out of New Zealand before they would let us on the plane from Melbourne to Auckland.

CHAPTER 36

The gentle years

Soon after, I landed in a beautiful new clinic with friendly and competent staff and a healthy work schedule in Elgin, Scotland. After all the years of working the system in Australia I knew my Angels had taken me out of that and into a softer and more caring environment.

I am wearing my uniform - bush green scrubs and blue plastic clogs. On my left shoe I have drawn two hearts and on the right VVT (the abbreviation for my name).

This croc identification process was done to prevent someone else wearing my clogs during open abdominal surgery or from just leaving their personal smell in them.. They would never smell the same after that kind of surgery.

The lack of unpleasant odour was one of the many reasons I had chosen ophthalmology. Eyes don't smell. They even don't bleed during the modern small incision form of cataract surgery. I had enjoyed most surgery, but particularly this detailed and careful form.

Scrub brush, antiseptic soap, and automated waterspouts: here we are again scrubbing! Scrubbing is very important and it is second nature to all surgeons. I have been doing this for a whole 30 years before performing or assisting surgery.

Behind me four nurses, in similar green scrubs, are busy preparing the theatre. The main scrub nurse, all gowned up with a face mask and latex gloves, plugs in the plastic tubing for irrigation and aspiration into the phaco emulsification machine.

Five minutes earlier, we had a brief. I was asked about the five patients on the list for this session. In order to avoid crucial mistakes such as operating on the wrong eye or implanting an incorrect lens, we confirmed the order in which the patients would be brought to theatre, the side to be operated on, as well as the appropriate lens strength. Any health or eye related risks are discussed and anticipated.

As I scrub I do my usual ritual. I pray.

As always I start praying to God, the universal creator and the Angels for a good outcome for all patients. I was so confident and so strong in my ability to trust the Angels that this was the first time I handed the surgery completely over to them.

"You guide me," I told them. "I will step back."

But that day things went wrong.

It was the day I completely surrendered to the higher source and opened up myself for the universal energy to flow through me.

That was the worst surgery of my life. Patient after patient things went wrong:

One elderly patient moved while I had instruments in his eye.
The phaco machine stopped working in the middle of the lens removal.
I was handed the wrong instruments.
A cannula jumped off in the eye during an injection.
Air bubbles obstructed my view of the lens.
The staff members were gossiping out loud about hating their job and manager's planning.
They criticised every instrument I asked for.
The incision was too small.
One lens unfolded upside down....

It was a litany of disasters! For a week I pondered what had gone wrong. It played on my mind all day.

A week later I started again to scrub for my surgery.

Scrub brush, antiseptic soap, automated waterspouts.

Scrub brush, antiseptic soap, automated waterspouts.

Scrub brush, antiseptic soap, automated waterspouts.

But this time I was angry. I was confused.

I tried my usual routine. I went into a trance.

I visualised all the machinery, instruments and staff working without fail. This time, however, something shifted. I stopped my usual out of body trance experience. I was fuming.

I sank back into my human vessel and I decided to have a difficult conversation with God.

This was very unlike me. I had not confronted God or my angelic helpers ever before. I asked God once to save me in the sea in South Africa.

Usually I choose peace over conflict. But this time I felt an unstoppable drive to confront God and the Angels.

My mind was on last week's surgery when almost all the patients' operations went haywire.

So I told them:

"Today … leave me alone. Don't help me. Don't interfere. I don't need you."

That day was the first time I told the Angels NOT to get involved in the surgery. I believed I would get back to good results by being completely present and not inviting them to assist or support.

But my Angels responded strangely to being put off. They said no.

No! We helped you always and we will continue. We have always been there, helping. But much of our helping has been to allow you to gather the skills you have. Your calling is to use the knowledge of science which we supported you to learn.

Who do you think guided you to and through medical school? Who stood by you all those long days in auditoriums? Who kept you company through all those late nights of memorizing for all the exams?

Who helped gathering information? Who was there while years of training and practice was provided to you?

You did not do this alone Veerle!

But you cannot hand over your role to anyone. You are the surgeon. The skills are yours, supported by us. The power is in your hands; supported by the knowledge and experience we helped you gather.

We will be here. But it is you who will do the physical surgery to the best of your ability. Not us!

This was a remarkable conversation to have. I saw its truth immediately. I had expected them to do my work for me too!

My head cleared and my anger left. I stood up and I knew what to do. I knew their roles in my surgery, and I knew mine. I scrubbed up with the nurses behind me and I resumed my prayers, knowing I would bring all I had gathered to my surgery that day. And I would use my own skills to make it happen. They would be standing right behind me the whole time.

CHAPTER 37

Angel messages vs intuition- how do you know?

I am often asked, how do I know it's an Angel? Could it just be my own inner voice or intuition?

The feeling is very different. Angel energy very clearly comes from outside but intuition comes from my belly.

I will give you an example to illustrate the difference. Once in South Africa we were in a private game reserve with a private ranger. We were in the car and the ranger wanted to get us closer to a big herd of 20 buffalo. He wanted to show us a good time. We got out of the car and we were walking closer and closer and I was feeling uncomfortable. Inside me there was a huge protest in my belly yelling: "No, no, this is too dangerous! Go back to the "car!"

It was overwhelming and powerful. I had to speak up. I knew it was not right.

Then I saw a footprint that I absolutely knew was from a lion.

"No," said the ranger, "it's a baboon." I said to Mark: "I am going back. I have a really bad feeling." My heart was pounding.

Now this is intuition.

Intuition is a basic instinct that speaks for your survival: We are reading all these signs and this is not safe for you. Go!

Mark listened.

"I know you well enough to know that if you say this, it is serious. Let's go!"

We turned around and raced back to the jeep and the guide followed us. I got to the jeep and saw two lionesses sitting there. One was waiting in front of the jeep and one behind. I ran to the car and jumped in. Mark got there, and then the ranger. He grabbed his gun, shocked. The next instant about 20 buffaloes tore around the corner toward the car. They split like the red sea against the side of the jeep. A third lioness behind them herded the group. It was a well set up hunting plan. They tore past the jeep, surprised, and ran on.

We sat in the Jeep reeling.

Mark was really angry with the ranger. We could have been killed.

CHAPTER 38

Angels I work with

In contrast, I had no fear whatsoever during the motorbike accident. I was in the greatest danger and yet Angels carried me. I knew I was safe. I was just curious what was going to happen. With Angels there is never a feeling of fear. It is only a feeling of love and safety.

The Angels I work with every day are Archangels Michael and Raphael and Gabriel.

Whenever I call upon Angels, they show up immediately. I call them silently, by name, in my head. Anyone can do that. Sometimes I ask to fill a treatment room or surgery with a thousand Angels to make the atmosphere more loving and to lift the vibration.

When I call on Angels I feel as if someone is embracing me. I feel the warmth and love. Angels feel as if they stand behind me and fold their wings around me. I see then with my inner eye.

Archangel Michael feels safe and warm to me. His colour is blue and in a relaxed state I see him as a dark blue-purple light.

He wraps his wings around me as protective shields. I call on him as protection against lower energies. I use his armour all over my body or his blue cloak and/or shield. Michael has protected me in dark cities, while being chased by creeps. He has miraculously saved me from drowning and from other near-death experiences. He carried me in his wings when I flew off the motorbike.

I also call on Raphael. He is my trusted helper in any healing or surgery I do.
I call him before starting any surgery. I ask him directly
"Archangel Raphael, please help me and the patient to get the best possible outcome from this operation I am about to do."

There are different Angels for different tasks.

For many years now I have invoked Angels to stand at the four corners of my property and one on the rooftop. I also drove my car in Australia with a very big red Angel on top of the roof to make me extra visible to the other traffic. It has kept me accident free but not parking ticket free! I should ask the parking ticket Angel to make my car invisible to parking attendants.

Entities I work with

In energy healing I remove the dark sick energy (often caused by negative emotions like anger and fear or negative thoughts by oneself or others). I prefer to remove the dark energy out of the patient's energy field before it gets stuck in the body, and before it causes physical damage. It can be removed in one session when it is new. It might take psychic surgery to cut out dark energies (these can also be entities inside the body and organs) before they cause cancer or other diseases.

The Spirit Guides I work with

The three spirit guides that have been with me the longest are a North American chief, a Chinese herbalist and an African fertility goddess.

My oldest spirit guide is Chief Longneck of the Navajo. The Navajo is a tribe still living in the Monument Valley Navajo National Park in Arizona, Utah.

He has come to me most of my life. He is a tall, strong man. He always stands straight, with his arm muscles tense and crossed across his naked, muscled torso. He doesn't feel approachable and doesn't talk much. I can't remember him ever smiling. His energy feels familiar like a younger person. He likes action, is very direct and talks in short sentences. His dark long hair is shiny and his eyes are brown. He wears a leather loincloth. His narrowed eyes glare intensely; his feet stand apart in power pose.

I first started feeling him after a strange visit to the Reserve in my twenties. I was with a group of four friends visiting the Navajo Reserve. As we arrived at the gates there was a large group of Navajo waiting. They walked straight up to me and singled me out.

"Chief," they said, "we have been waiting for you. We welcome you back."

We all stood bug-eyed. What was going on? I was a normal girl in shorts and aerobics shoes and they were welcoming me as a chief. That freaked me out at the time. They wanted me to go with them but I was too scared to leave my friends and to go with a group of strange men.

"The chief wants to see you," they insisted. I was equally insistent. I was not going anywhere alone. They got very agitated but eventually accepted and waved us into the park with an angry flick of their hands. But they tried to insist I come with them our entire visit.

A few hours later my eyes were drawn up and I saw him sitting there. Their current chief was sitting on a white horse up on one of the natural sandstone rocks. He was watching me. I turned away, my heart racing.

It was a while later that I started to notice my spirit guide. Chief Longneck has taught me how to connect with nature. It is also thanks to this guide that I can read nature, the weather, the ocean, the wind and the earth. He is my physically strong, earthly helper. His greatest gift is that I can lovingly heal animals and humans with my hands. He helps me to improve my intuition and instinct.

He is there when I need physical strength: he loves it when I run or ride a horse. Lately he keeps on saying to me: "Go to the gym!" as he disapproves of my flabby arms. He has been there for me in many events where my life was in danger. Despite of my myopic eyesight, I have a guardian who warns me.

My second guide is an old Chinese herbalist with a soft, gentle smile, wise eyes, a bald head and a long narrow light grey beard. He showed me his medicinal cabinet once, during a meditation. It had heaps of little drawers, filled with dried plants and who knows what: dried toads, rhino horn and ginger root. I am not sure how long he has been with me but possibly many lifetimes, as I have been a healer in several lives before this one.

I have been attracted to Chinese medicine: acupuncture and shiatsu massage and foot reflexology for many decennia.

I actually studied Feng Shui and designed the ideal house around that. I have benefitted many times from moving rooms, bed directions, the position of my desk at work and the chair I choose at the meeting table. The year I was diagnosed with heart disease was a bad year for the mother of the house. The year Mark died was the year the father of the house's life was in danger. I told Mark this, and ordered him a protective amulet that he could attach to his keyring but he refused to carry it with him.

My third spirit guide is an African earth goddess. She has many fat rolls, laughs out loud and keeps on saying to me that I should have more babies. She helped with the conception of my three healthy children when I was between 35 and 41 years old (despite my husband being diagnosed with very low active sperm count). She was an African medicine woman, naked apart from a grass skirt.

CHAPTER 39
Meditations and processes to connect to other beings

The Clairs and how to connect to other beings

There are seven main recognised Clairs: Clairvoyance (vision), Clairsentience (feeling), Clairaudience (hearing), Clairalience (smell), Clair cognisance (knowing), Clairgustance (tasting), Clairvocalising (speaking). There is also Precognition and Telepathy.

Clairvoyance

Some people can see spirits or light beings directly. But I see Angels as different colours. I see dark green for Archangel Raphael, blue for Archangel Michael and dark purple for Metatron (a recent angel to visit me). They look like moving energy blobs like the ones in lava lamps but bigger. I see them better with my third eye, when my eyes are closed and when I am quiet and relaxed - like during a meditation.

Clairaudience

Sometimes I hear very clear advice in my head. "Don't go in this alley, it is dangerous" or "Cross the street now". I know this is a voice from outside. Angels would never tell you to do anything that is not based on love. You always have free will.

Bad advice such as, "Drive your car against that post in order to kill yourself" doesn't ever come from Angels. There are, however, some negative entities and mischievous spirits on the earthly plane that might try to cause havoc.

Clairsentience

When I am in the presence of Angels I consistently feel a warm, loving, caring presence. I feel safe like I am enrobed in their big angel wings.

During my early childhood, as I used to astral travel around the world and through the universes, I was always aware of a being by my side.

I couldn't see or hear him, but felt him. Equally when I walked home in the dark from music school an Angel held my left hand all the way home. If it doesn't feel good, it is not an Angel! If it gives goose bumps or chills it is a spirit or ghost. Even chairs and rooms can have a negative imprinted energy left behind.

A homeopath was testing me one day and I was sitting on the usual patient chair. I felt very uncomfortable. All the diseased energy that had been left behind by previous patients was very real to me. It felt sticky, and I could feel dark and heavy treads latching onto my back as he was muscle-testing me using kinesiology for diagnosis.

I tested positive for all diseases under the rainbow. The technician had not seen anything like this before. He scratched his head.

"You even test positive for prostate cancer," he said. Clearly I don't have a prostrate because I am female.

I knew I had absorbed all the sick energy into my own aura and his machine measured it.

"It's this chair," I said. "I want to move to another chair and let's do it again."

He agreed and he retested me. The measurements were a lot more relevant for me.

I didn't really like the fact that imprints could influence the test results so easily. I never went back there.

I have learned how to close my energy field fast once I pick up on these phenomena. The Purple Flame is the best cleansing visualisation that you can call in to clear these out of your field. It is described in the next section.

Claircognisance

I know things without knowing how I know it. This helped me through medical school and with diagnoses with patients. I knew what was wrong without any tests. During written exams I always feel calm and surrounded by my Angels as well as spirit guides (previous doctors/ healers) and the answers often flowed out of my pen, as they do now.

Clairalience

Sometimes I pick up smells coming from high vibrational beings, present in the room.

Quan Yin, a buddhist deity, who had earned entrance to Nirvana, chose to stay close to earth to help more humans ascend and to bring relief to the suffering (some consider her the female Buddha). In my experience her presence is accompanied by the scent of jasmine flowers.
Mother Mary also has a flowery smell like roses.

Sometimes the smell even wakes me up. I also had a period where I smelled the cigars my decades-dead grandfather had been smoking. He visited me often at night when I was a small child. When I described him to my father as the tall, skinny man with a raincoat and a hat and glasses, he knew I was talking about his father. I only discovered this years later, when I found an old portrait of my grandfather and recognised him.

Sometimes I still wake from the smell of burning wood and I think that is one of my stamina spirit guides visiting me at night. When we sleep, these beings are often actually working on us: given us useful thoughts, solving our problems in our dreams our doing energy healing on our bodies. When we sleep we are quite open and vulnerable. That's why I like to pray at night. I always ask God and the Angels to surround me with a protective cocoon of white divine light. That keeps the nightmares and creepy entities out.

The Angels can still work on you, as they often do, while you sleep in your protective bubble.

Clairvocal

I do not speak or channel the words of others, but sometimes I blurt out things to people. I used to do that quite often: speak the truth to fakes and dishonest folks. I couldn't help it. This didn't make me popular, as you can imagine.

My tone of voice and the way I speak is clearly different to my friends when I do this.

My friends tell me that when this happens my voice changes. It appears that messages flow through me from a higher source. They also notice when I snap out of it and become normal, earthly, ordinary Veerle again.

Age has taught me to control what I say. I stick to the Flemish advice: Don't throw your pearls to the swine.

This means: Don't offer your precious insights and advice to people who are not ready to hear it.

CHAPTER 40

Techniques to connect and call on Angels

There are some techniques that I have used for many years, and also that I recommend my patients use for healing or before undergoing an operation. All of these, however, can be used any time to call in a higher energy, into any situation.

Most prayers are made of simple stuff. They focus on what is good and right, and call on the best and the good to support you and help. It doesn't matter whether you pray to God, the Angels, Source, or any other forms of higher consciousness. Just call on who you feel is good and right.

When you open up to spirits or pray, set the clear intention to only connect to benevolent beings. They have a high love vibration and would never make you feel fearful or angry. These beings have the high energy of love, gratitude and above.

A prayer before undergoing surgery

Do this as you sit in the doctor's room or lie in the operation theatre:
Close your eyes.
Still your mind and breathe slowly and deeply.
Call on Angels or your God or Higher Self to allow only positive energy to enter the room. Ask the Ideal Healing Angels to fill the room and stay with you through the whole procedure and recovery.
Fill yourself up with their white divine light.
Surround yourself with a white cocoon of light.
Let the light fill the entire room.
Silently, or out loud, ask your God to let all the people in this room work towards the best possible result and outcome.
"May all the people in this room work towards the best possible outcome.
May everything go smoothly and according to plan.
May everyone in this room be filled with healing light."
Visualise yourself walking out in radiant health.

How to clear a room of bad energy

You can also use the above technique to alter or change a scary environment. I use this technique even when I walk into a room or space that has bad energy.
I just surround myself with Angels.
When there are bad tempered people present, I call on the Peace Angels to fill the whole room. Most of the time, the low vibration people will leave and those left are the people who can change and feel comfortable with the higher vibration surrounding them.

When you feel bad vibes in a space or around people, the other option is for you to just leave.

If I walk into a place (often a casino or a bar, a battlefield or old prison) where there is bad energy, I just turn around and leave. I don't bother to call on the angels. I had to learn to do that. Originally I was attracted to ALL ENERGY. I couldn't feel the difference between light and dark. It took me a long time to learn. Now I feel it straight away. I can feel it in people or things. I try to steer clear of all negativity in my life. Seek out what feels light and loving – that's where you go.

Techniques to Clear a New Space

When moving into a new space, house, office or even a hotel room, you can clear the energy left behind using a number of techniques. I use these often after I have performed surgery or healing. However, you have to be careful to choose one that is compliant with health regulations!

USING SMOKE

The most common way to clear a space is to use white sage. Dry out a bunch of sage or buy it dried. Then light the sage on a plate so it smoulders. Then walk through your space and let the smoke fill all the corners. Use your hand to move it into all the spaces. Open the windows so the smoke can leave with the unwanted spirits or imprints.

You can also clear a space using incense. I carry this in my bag and always use some in hotel rooms. Hold the highest intention while you hold the smoking stick in your hand that all energies left behind get cleared out and replaced with love, peace, harmony and health.

ROSE QUARTZ

As a protection you can also place rose quartz crystals all over your space. I use these regularly and often clear a surgery using these. All the beds in my house have a large rose quartz underneath so only love can enter. It helps to keep worries and nightmares away.

SOUND

Put on some music that has a higher vibration. Find some meditation music or chants. Any clear, natural sound works wonders. I love the sound of waterfalls, the rain and the beach. Wind chimes also chase away evil spirits as do the chiming of metal bells and singing bowls. You may want to combine the burning of sage with a bell that you ring at the same time, or even a song you sing with joy and love.

A meditation for post-operative healing

This is a great way to energise your body to heal, repair and recover.

Lie or sit still
Hold your silence and space.
Breathe deeply and close your eyes.
Slow your breathing.
Connect with a pure beautiful light 100 metres above you.
This is the same place you contact when praying.
Feel your soul chakra.
This sits about one meter higher than your crown chakra above your head.

Let a beautiful pure light come in through your soul chakra.
Let the light flood down over you.
Let it move through you and connect with the earth chakra about a metre below your feet.
Let it flow through you down into the centre of the earth.
Feel it connecting to the centre of the earth.
Feel the real unconditional mother's love and support.
Notice this feeling in the centre of our planet, which has been carrying you since the day you were born
Now imagine strong cables coming out through your feet, connecting to the centre of the planet.
See them like hollow straws.
Let them suck up the hot, red lava
This lava is full of energising Kundalini life energy.
Imagine it running up through your feet, into your legs and into your spine from your root chakra.
See it run all over your head and back down into the earth through the front of your body and out your feet.

The Energetic Vomit

If you are ever feeling that you are toxic with negative emotions try this. This manoeuvre works miracles to release that negative energy (without causing a mess).

Chose a private place and sit quietly
Close your eyes.
Allow yourself to feel all the negative energy in your body.
Try and feel all the places it lives and rests.
Draw these feelings towards your solar plexus
Let them gather there.
Feel them flow and condense there.
If you can, put a name to them.
Sit with the feeling in your stomach as it grows and swirls.
When you are ready to release this you can start to make actual physical noises.
You may make a retching noise, or a series of deep choking breaths.
You may find you actually want to physically vomit.
Allow this to happen.
Make a noise from your mouth.
Allow it to end when you are ready.

Sit quietly for a while and notice the energy change.
Notice how easy it is to let these feelings go.
Allow yourself to feel free of them.
Allow yourself to feel light and open.
Seal your practice with silence as you thank yourself, your Angels and your God.

The Purple Flame

This is a technique to clear unwanted energies from your body. I often use this and most often when I am taking a shower at the end of the day before bed. It is very useful after a surgery, or a day with patients all offloading their own stuff.

Imagine a Violet flame starting to form a rotating vortex under the soles of your feet.

Imagine this as a highly powerful intelligence.

It has the power to transform.
It has the power to wash away all the dark energy you might have picked up during the day.
See it rising from your feet and up over your body in a swirling motion.
See it lifting the unwanted energy up into the sky where higher beings will take care of it.
Let it leave your body and rise away.
Be grateful that you feel so much lighter now.

Rain Shower Ritual

You can actually do this ritual in the shower or just take an imaginary shower of rainbow colours. Or you can do this during a walk outdoors. I also have different lights in my spa bath that change colour. I sit in it and absorb the vibration of the colour.

Imagine a loving bright white light filling you up through the top of your head and shining through your eyes so that you can actually SEE Love and Truth.
Let ears fill up with the divine light so that you can only HEAR Love and Truth.
Let your throat fill up with the universal white light so that you can only SPEAK with Love and Truth.
Allow the Light to fill your Heart so you can only FEEL Love and Truth.
Fill yourself with Love, Truth and Light.
Let the light surround you like an exhaled cocoon, and wash away all negative energies.

Let the Light fill up your Solar Plexus (stomach area) where you feel fear. Wash this dark energy away with the bright light like a waterless waterfall.

Sometimes, fear or hurt can make you feel nauseous.

If you feel nausea then do an Energetic Vomit.

When you have filled up your stomach area with the Divine Light, inviting more Truth, Light and Love, you will feel balanced, happy and connected. Heaven and earth energy connect in the solar plexus.

Then let the Light move down into your Earth Star, about a metre under your feet. This is the area that MOVES you into you truth so you can feel secure and grounded.
If you feel you need to add more colours go with it. I find red very powerful for physical strength and determination and orange for creativity and fun. Yellow improves your willpower. Green and pink serve Jesus and Love.

Turquoise stimulates honest communication. Indigo opens your third eye for clarity. Purple connects you to your higher self.

Move the light down into your thighs, knees, calves, ankles and feet, all the way into your Earthstar.

Add any colour that intuitively feels right to you.

Expand your Earthstar, which is situated about 30cm to a metre below your feet.
From there you can easily connect to the centre of the planet.

I spontaneously see a two-pointed quartz crystal and cords coming out of the soles of my feet to connect to both poles of the crystal.
When you feel connected to Mother Earth in the centre of GAIA, you feel happy, safe and secure.
Allow this crystalline energy from the centre of the earth to move up your legs, hips, abdomen, and chest filling you up with supportive safe strength.

Let the energy squirt out of the top of your crown like a beautiful fountain with sparkles of gold or silver and any colour you fancy to fill your aura.

I first really understood the power of this ritual one particular day in Springwood, Queensland during the last Christmas holiday Mark and I had with our three young children in Lamington National Park. One day between Christmas and New Year 2011 my whole family walked much faster than I expected down the 300 steps of the walking trail that took us into the canyon. My little Angels ran down, smoothly drawn by gravity.

Mark was slower and looked less energetic than usual. We didn't know yet but the cancer was eating the life out of him. But he still protected his roost and waited for me. I was the slowest. I had injured my left knee when I had kicked a foot pedal and had torn my meniscus during cataract surgery. At the bottom you can walk under a waterfall. When the light splits into the colour of the rainbow I felt power everywhere. There were ions everywhere. It was a cleansing bath of water and rainbow colours. These colours all represent different energies. As I stood there I called Mark back. I told him to stand there to heal and cleanse. I could just feel it. But he refused to do it. Often he refused my advice in life! It was his choice all the way.

A meditation to remember self-love

Remember a time in your life that you were the happiest. It could be when you were a six-year-old child playing with a kitten. It could be a disco party with friends. Your first love, your first child or car or pay cheque....

For me it is a memory of being healthy and young and slim and loved, walking on a beach in South Africa with my feet in the fresh Indian Ocean and the warm sun on my tanned skin. I felt so grateful to be alive at that moment.

Now sit or lie in a relaxed position in a quiet place and see yourself traveling back to that happy moment in time.

What did you look like? What were you wearing? Who was with you? What was your environment like? Feel the emotions running through your body. Where do you feel happy, elated, and so full of joy?

Is it in your heart or your tummy or somewhere else? Feel this, what colour does it have? What sounds do you hear? What does it taste like?

Step into that picture. What are you thinking? What do you see, hear and feel?

Breathe in the happiness into every cell of your body and breathe out any stressful feelings.
Breathe in love, breathe out anger.
Breathe in joy, breathe out sadness.
Breathe in a white light, breath out darkness.
Allow the light to fill every part of your body from head to toe.
Keep repeating this until every part of your body is filled with this healing, protective light.
Expand the white light into a cocoon around your body.
Now ask your younger version: "What should I do, so I can keep this happiness with me for the rest of my life?"

Be open to receiving the answer. It could be a clear instruction, an image, or a feeling.

Accept it gracefully and say to your younger self: "Thank you. Please forgive me if I ever let you down. I promise to honour you and our joy and our life for every day from here on."

Enjoy a last moment in the happiest time of your life and bring that energy into your present. Jump up and tell someone you love how much they mean to you. Ask them to do something FUN, something you have always wanted to do but never prioritised because you were too busy taking care of others or providing for your family, patients or clients.

Write down your promise to yourself.

Take one step towards your goal NOW!